# The Social Life of the Early Modern Protestant Clergy

Special Issue of
*The Journal of Religious History, Literature and Culture*
2020

*Edited by*
JACQUELINE EALES and BEVERLY TJERNGREN



Volume 6 November 2020 Number 2
UNIVERSITY OF WALES PRESS
*https://doi.org/10.16922/jrhlc.6.2*

# CONTENTS

# THE CONTRIBUTORS

**Jacqueline Eales** is Professor Emeritus at Canterbury Christ Church University, where she worked for twenty-seven years and was the founding Director of the Centre for Kent History and Heritage. Her specialist areas of research include Puritanism, The English Civil Wars and Early Modern Women's History. She was President of the Historical Association from 2011–14.

**William Gibson** is Professor of Ecclesiastical History and Director of the Oxford Centre for Methodism and Church History at Oxford Brookes University.

**Jonas Lindström** holds a PhD in history and is a researcher at the Department of History, Uppsala University. His work focuses on early modern rural society and the gender division of work.

**Rosamund Oates** is a Reader in History at Manchester Metropolitan University, and works on early modern religious cultures. Her research interests cover preaching, deafness, reading history and clerical families. Recent publications include *Moderate Radical: Tobie Matthew and the English Reformation* (Oxford, 2018) and *Communities of Print: Readers and their Books in Early Modern Europe* (Brill, 2021, with Jessica Purdy).

**Jon Stobart** is Professor of History at Manchester Metropolitan University. His research interests span a range of topics in the history of retailing, consumption and material culture, most recently in the context of the English country house. This has led to a number of publications, most notably *Consumption and the Country House* (Oxford University Press, 2016, with Mark Rothery), and the edited collections *Travel and the British Country House* (Manchester University Press, 2017) and *The Comforts of Home in Western Europe, 1700–1900* (Bloomsbury, 2020).

**Beverly Tjerngren** is a PhD student at the Department of History, Uppsala University. Her research focuses on rural clergy in early modern Sweden.

# EDITORIAL

The articles in this special issue are based on the authors' presentations at the European Social Science History Conference in Belfast on 5 April 2018. They were presented in a double session conceived and organized by Beverly Tjerngren, with considerable and generous advice and assistance from Jon Stobart. The two panels, under the common heading 'The Man Behind the Curtain: The Social Life of the Clergy', explored the lives of early modern English and Swedish clergy outside their official duties in a church setting. The first session focused largely on said clergymen's economic conditions and possibilities while the second centred around the phenomenon of the clerical family. The articles are presented here in a roughly chronological order, rather than in the order of conference presentation.

Three of the contributions focus on the new phenomenon of clerical marriage after the Reformation. Rosamunde Oates argues that in England the first generations of clergy wives used their obligations of hospitality to engage actively in the process of reform. This was evident both in the households of bishops and in the homes of the parish clergy. Jacqueline Eales examines the shift from a general defence of clerical marriage by the English clergy to the positive portrayal of individual clergy wives and daughters, who were increasingly depicted as exemplary role models in the century from 1620 to 1720. Beverly Tjerngren provides a case study of an eighteenth-century Swedish clerical marriage and charts the decline of hospitality in the pastor's parish home after the death of his wife.

The other three contributions centre on the economic and financial status of the clergy. William Gibson challenges the view that the eighteenth century English episcopate were greedy for preferment and illustrates their efforts to safeguard the estates of their bishoprics sometimes drawing on their personal income to do so. Far from being rapacious, these church leaders were often careful custodians of the church finances entrusted to them. Jonas Lindström provides a case study of the economic networks of an eighteenth century Swedish pastor and demonstrates how parishioners and clergy were bound not just by religious and social ties, but by their economic relationships as well.

Jon Stobart examines the domestic material culture of a group of rural Northamptonshire clergy in the late eighteenth and early nineteenth centuries. He concludes that these men and their families aspired to gentility through their domestic settings, which aligned them to the social, cultural and material worlds of the gentry.

The participants would like to thank discussants Janine Maegraith (University of Vienna) and Mikael Alm (Uppsala University) for their helpful and insightful comments during the panel presentations in Belfast.

A version of Jacqueline Eales's contribution was read in October 2019 at a symposium on the Clerical Estate at Lincoln College, Oxford, in honour of Dr Andrew Foster. We also extend special thanks to Dr Foster for reading and commenting on the articles.

We are also grateful to William Gibson for organising the publication of this special issue of the JRHL&C. His guiding hand has led us graciously and ably through the process from start to finish as we collected and edited the articles for this volume.

With much appreciation,
Jacqueline Eales and Beverly Tjerngren

# MARTHA OR MARY? CLERICAL WIVES AND HOSPITALITY IN THE ENGLISH REFORMATION

Rosamund Oates, Manchester Metropolitan University

'In 1575, someone in the Elizabethan government drew up a parliamentary bill designed to reform clerical hospitality. The author complained that 'diverse of the clergy now being married, and having wife and children, do over much alienate their minds from the honest and careful duties . . . of good hospitality'. The bill never made it beyond the draft stage, but it illustrates the importance of clerical hospitality to the Elizabethan regime and fears about wifely influence in clerical households. The author attacked the fairly new practice of clerical marriage, claiming that wives exercised too much power in clerical households, particularly large episcopal households. Wives, he complained, should not 'intrude' into the 'worldly affairs of any such seat of government as now far otherwise at present is reported'. Instead, the bill proposed to increase hospitality by forbidding clerical wives to have anything 'to do in any respect with the order, rule of government of the household'. Women were ordered to concentrate on educating children, and on 'godly exercises' such as 'prayer, alms deeds and ministering to the poor'. In the 1575 act, the professional and pastoral aspects of the clerical household – namely hospitality – were to be restricted to the clergyman himself.[1]

The bill of 1575 was not presented to parliament, but it reflects both the influence that clerical wives could have in the Church of England and contemporary unease about it. Clerical marriage was one of the most significant innovations of the Reformation and historians have explored how contemporaries, from parishioners to Queen Elizabeth, responded to clerical marriage.[2] Little attention, however, has been paid to how far clerical wives in England were agents of change. Marriage to clergymen offered women a degree of agency in the Church, allowing them to take an active, and influential, role in the 'Protestantisation' of England.[3]

https://doi.org/10.16922/jrhlc.6.2.1

Motivated by a genuine commitment to Evangelical reform, many clerical wives saw themselves as active participants in the establishment of the Church of England. Women could discharge their husbands' pastoral duties through the 'public housekeeping' of the household (most notably hospitality), and they wielded further influence through the soft power of convivial dining and networks of kin and friendship that shaped the post-Reformation Church in England. Historians have asked, 'was there a Reformation for women', and at least part of that answer lies in the experiences of clerical wives in the vicarages, deaneries and episcopal palaces of early modern England.[4]

This article demonstrates the influence of clerical wives in the Elizabethan and Jacobean Church by focussing on networks of patronage around the two centres of the Church in northern England: Durham and York. The experiences of Frances Matthew *née* Barlow (1550/1–1629), married to archbishop of York, Tobie Matthew (*c.*1544–1628), highlights the influence of wives who had the resources of the clerical household at their disposal. Mary Prior has argued that bishops' wives had limited authority in the episcopal households of the sixteenth and seventeenth centuries. However, as Frances Matthew's experience shows the provision of hospitality – an important clerical duty – was a sphere which episcopal wives could, and did, control.[5] This potentially gave them great influence, giving rise to the anxiety seen in the parliamentary bill drafted in 1575. This was particularly true for the families of senior clerics, who had inherited a medieval tradition of hospitality akin to that expected of the gentry and nobility. And hospitality was important in the success of the English Reformation. Felicity Heal and Kenneth Fincham have both shown that hospitality was a significant part of the episcopal role in the Elizabethan and Jacobean Church.[6]

This article is not just about the influence that women exercised through the households of their clerical husbands, but also about perceptions of the ideal clerical wife in the period. Discussions about clerical hospitality were a flashpoint for larger arguments about the role, power and status of clerical wives. Contemporaries like the author of the 1575 bill tried to argue that clerical wives could be involved only in household activities that had no professional element, restricting them to female activities such as personal devotion and the education of children. Although it was the hospitality of senior clerics that came under the closest scrutiny, these debates had relevance for all clerical wives as contemporaries discussed whether wives should help husbands with their pastoral duties or withdraw into a private piety. Contemporaries used the biblical story of two sisters – Mary and Martha of Bethany – to contrast alternative models of female piety. When Jesus visited their home, Martha rushed around providing food and drink for their guest while Mary sat at Jesus's feet, listening quietly. Even supporters of clerical marriage often shied away from celebrating wifely involvement in hospitality, aware of how contentious the topic could be. Although preachers praised Martha's 'good husbandry', clerical and lay wives were told to aspire to Mary's private devotions and to keep out of household affairs.[7] For many clerical households, however the reality was very different.

Clerical marriage was a significant innovation in early modern England, creating a new class of women who did not have a clear template of behaviour, at least for the first decades of Elizabeth's reign. The earliest discussions about an ideal minister's wife were focussed on her moral and sexual probity. After clerical marriage was legalised in 1559, a potential bride needed two letters testifying to her 'good fame and name' before bishops could issue a license to allow the marriage. The injunction was designed to avoid scandal, and as Anne Thompson has shown, the practice continued into the seventeenth century, sustaining a continued interest in the moral rectitude of clerical wives. This emphasis on sexual probity reflected polemical disputes about the value of clerical marriage, with the earliest Protestant writers justifying marriage as an alternative to clerical concubinage.[8] In the 1540 bestseller, *De Christlich Eestand* (translated as *The Christen State of Matrimonie*), Heinrich Bullinger defended clerical marriage with the argument that: 'the saying of Paul endureth unmoveable: it is better to marry than burn'. In his book defending clerical marriage, *An Apologie Fully Answering . . . Thomas Martin* (1566), John Ponet expanded Paul's dictum to argue that sexual corruption led to spiritual error, writing 'the first infectors of Christendom with erroneous opinions were unmarried priests'. Reading Ponet's book in Elizabethan Durham, Bishop Tobie Matthew (himself married), wrote a note in the margins: 'heresie and lecherie [are] ioyned together'.[9] Clerical marriage was to stand as the opposite of both, and throughout the period there was a sustained interest in the sexual standing of clerical wives. In 1609, William Perkins stressed that ministers must not marry 'a harlot . . . though she be repentant' because it 'may prejudice the dignity and respect' of the ministry and successive Elizabethan and Jacobean visitation articles enquired if the clergy lived with women who were reported to be 'incontinent'.[10]

More positive templates of clerical marriage, however, were hard to find for the first generations of clerical wives. The Bible was an obvious source, and Protestant reformers were keen to assert that clerical marriage was a biblical tradition. Bullinger reminded his readers that priests in both the Old and New Testaments were married.[11] Ponet repeated this in *An Apologie*, and his copy Tobie Matthew recorded that: 'Bishops and Priests in the Primitive Churche had wives, who were called Episcopa and Presbyterae'. Further on Matthew wrote a note to himself that St Peter had had a wife. When Matthew Parker oversaw the publication of *A Defence of Priests Marriage* in 1567, he also reminded readers that the apostles were married. St Paul's letter to Timothy, in which Paul compared the Church to the house of God, was a particularly useful source of inspiration for married ministers. Paul required clerical wives to 'be honest, not evil speakers, but sober and faithful in all things'. Furthermore, he drew parallels between the well-ordered household and the Church, ordering a bishop or deacon 'to rule his own house honestly, having children under obedience', asking, 'if any cannot rule his own house, how shall he care for the Church of God?'[12] What this meant in practice, however, was not always clear. Some believed that by promoting the household as a centre of faith, St Paul encouraged hospitality. In 1619, the clergyman John Favour praised Archbishop Tobie Matthew as being the ideal of the Pauline bishop, claiming that Matthew was 'diligent' in preaching and 'as affable in your entertainment'.[13]

Historians have recognised that in the earliest days of the Reformation clerical marriage reflected Evangelical beliefs, and even after clerical marriage was legal, marrying a clergyman continued to be a powerful statement of religious intent. One of the first clerical wives in England was Agnes Wellesburn, married to Bishop William Barlow during the reign of Henry VIII. Her children included Frances Matthew, who praised her mother's dedication to Protestantism in a memorial erected after 1595, celebrating Agnes's suffering in exile under Mary for 'gospel sake' and noting that she 'died in the Lord, whom she daily served'.[14] Clerical wives – particularly at the start of Elizabeth's reign – often had a deeply held commitment to Protestant reform. Bishop Richard Cox's second wife was a former Marian exile, Jane Turner, and Bishop Parkhurst's wife, Margaret, was in regular contact with Henrich Bullinger.[15] While clerical marriage became more normalised through Elizabeth's reign, it was still, however, one of the only ways in which women could exercise their Evangelical commitments. Into the seventeenth century, women continued to see marriage to clergy as offering a special position; it was reported that Elizabeth Gouge wanted to marry a minister: 'such respect did this gentlewoman bear to the Ministry of God's word'.[16]

When it came to fashioning the ideal clerical marriage, examples from the first decades of the European Reformation had a particular resonance, reflecting Evangelical ideas about clerical households. The most famous of these marriages was, of course, that of Martin and Katarina Luther, which was widely reported in pamphlets, letters, and publications of Luther's 'table talk'. Significantly, hospitality was at the heart of these family lives, with clerical wives providing the hospitality that sustained the early Reformation: Martin and Katarina Luther, and Martin and Elizabeth Bucer were renowned for playing host to students and supporters. In Edwardian England, English Protestants witnessed this vision of domestic Protestantism firsthand, with many English reformers marrying into Reformed families. [17] Those connections were further strengthened during the Marian exile, when clerics and their wives (like the Barlow family) were forced to rely on the hospitality of their continental counterparts. As a result, hospitality – an ancient tradition – acquired a specifically Protestant legacy in which wifely involvement was often praised. It was a legacy recalled by Caleb Dalechamp in 1632, when he praised the role played by Peter Martyr's wife in providing hospitality for 'persecuted and weather-beaten Christians'.[18]

From 1559, clerical marriage was an accepted feature of the Elizabethan Church. At the same time, hospitality – a medieval tradition – was recognized as an important duty of ministers, particularly the senior clerics who were responsible for establishing Protestantism. As hospitality became a key element in the proselytization of Elizabethan England, the clerical household came under increasing scrutiny – especially the households of deans, bishops and archdeacons who could afford the sort of hospitality that had political as well as charitable benefits. These households were often overseen by wives, many of whom were committed Protestants who could, and did, use their influence over the household to actively support their husbands' professional duties. This was not, however, a development that was universally embraced by contemporaries.

Hospitality had two elements in late medieval and early modern England: entertaining visitors and providing charity. Ideally, the two were combined, with food prepared for eminent guests later feeding the poor and needy. William Harrison portrayed a scene unchanged from the fifteenth century when he described a meal in a noble household. Harrison wrote that after the nobleman, his family and guests had eaten their fill, the remaining food was 'bestowed upon the poor, which lie ready at their gates', and a similar pattern was expected to take place in episcopal palaces.[19] Early supporters of the Church of England saw this powerful tradition of clerical hospitality as a way of winning support for the new regime. In 1559, the first Elizabethan visitors of Durham Cathedral reminded the canons of the importance of hospitality in their efforts to establish a Protestant Church. Matthew Parker, Elizabeth's first archbishop of Canterbury, echoed these concerns. Writing to William Cecil in 1563, Parker worried that if bishops and 'ordinary ministers' could not provide hospitality they would be 'brought to contempt for lack of reasonable necessities'. Cecil agreed, and throughout the period he supported hospitality as a powerful tool of persuasion. In notes written in 1585, Cecil wrote that bishops and clergy should 'specially by hospitality and relieving the poor, win credit among the people'. Where the clergy did not provide hospitality, Cecil wrote that they were 'rather despised than revered or beloved'.[20]

In 1582, when Tobie Matthew was appointed to the deanery of Durham, his first and most pressing issue was securing enough income to provide hospitality. Convivial dining and charitable donations were, in his eyes, essential to gain supporters in what was still a relatively hostile diocese. In the summer of 1582, before he was transferred north, Matthew was anxious about crops belonging to the deanery, warning that 'things there go to wrack' and worrying about 'provisions for the year following'. Later in August 1582, Matthew once again begged Cecil to let him move into the deanery before 'the whole crop, as well of hay and corn, as all other fruits' passed to the prebendaries, leaving him 'no provision whereith to keep house and so less able to do good in preaching or government'. He warned Cecil that 'many regard hospitality very much, who being lost at this first, will hardly be won a good while over'.[21]

When Matthew finally arrived in Durham in 1583, hospitality continued to pre-occupy him. The 1569 Northern Rebellion had revealed the extent of Catholicism in the diocese, and Matthew thought that hospitality would help him to win support among northerners and reconcile old enemies to the new regime. Tobie Matthew worked with the prebendaries to ensure that food and drink was provided for the poor from the dining hall in the cathedral, and he tried to enforce statutes which required cathedral clergy to provide their own charitable donations.

Meanwhile, Tobie and Frances Matthew made up any shortfall through their own household, with Francis Walsingham praising the extent of the hospitality provided in the deanery. Matthew assured his political patrons that he had been keeping detailed receipts and expected – or rather hoped – for reimbursement.[22]

All clerics shared the duty of hospitality, and the charity of parochial clergy was an important part of the local economy, particularly in times of need. Need was particularly acute in the 1590s, when a series of poor harvests led to widespread dearth and starvation. In 1596 the government responded to the famine by issuing a nationwide appeal for alms as part of a campaign of fasting and prayers; a royal proclamation ordered 'persons of ability' to keep away from London and 'to stay in their countries and keep hospitality'. The provision of food – and sometimes shelter – was often more valuable to starving men and women than money channelled through the poor box. Everyone, but particularly clergy, was encouraged to find food for starving neighbours.[23] 'Is this not the fast that pleaseth?' asked the author of homilies issued in 1596, 'to deal thy bread to the hungry'? Some clergy struggled to provide extra food and felt it keenly. Bernard Gilpin, of County Durham, found it increasingly hard to continue his regular commitment of providing dinner for his parishioners. In 1597, Dean William James reported on the continued and devastating effect of the famine in the diocese of Durham, warning that 'the poor are multiplied and hospitality, which was much regarded, [is] greatly decayed'. As a result, men and women were risking their lives by travelling to plague-ridden Newcastle to buy corn, 'as it were through fire and water'. Without the corn which was imported from Europe, James warned that: 'no man can express the misery that would ensue'.[24]

Many clergy increased their provision of hospitality in response to the famines of the 1590s. By the winter of 1596, the Dean and Chapter of Westminster were complaining to Robert Cecil that 'the maintenance of daily hospitality is grown to be so great, as without further present provision we can not be well able to continue it'. Up in Durham, Tobie Matthew continued his drive to increase clerical hospitality: as plague and starvation tore through the diocese, he wrote to William Cecil arguing that ministers who did not make 'so much relief to the poor by hospitality' should be thrown out of their livings and replaced by a 'sufficient minister'. His concerns were widespread. A couple of months later, Convocation approved a bill which reminded ministers to provide regular hospitality. At the bottom of his copy of the bill, William Cecil wrote a note: 'I have read and perused these constitutions and I think if they shall be well executed, the Church shall be well ordered'.[25] Throughout the period, clerical families were expected to provide the hospitality underpinning the social and economic interactions of the local community. In November 1649, after several years of bad harvests and war, the Essex minister Ralph Josselin and his wife decided to miss a couple of meals a week, so that they could give their food to poor neighbours.[26]

Conviviality, as well as charitable giving, underpinned hospitality, and could be part of a strategy of building support for the Church in the community. Caleb Dalechamp, dedicated his 1632 book *Christian Hospitality* to the single, and famously gregarious, bishop of Lincoln, John Williams, writing that hospitality was 'in a strict and accurate sense nothing else but the love that is born to strangers', and included 'the feasting of neighbours' as well as 'the relieving of the poor'.[27] Hospitality was used to reconcile local gentry opposed to the regime, many of whom were Catholics. When Matthew became bishop of Durham in 1595, he and his new dean, William James, started to invite 'the better sort' of Catholics into their households in an attempt to try and convert them. It was a well-recognised strategy, recommended by Peter Martyr Vermigli in his influential book, *Treatise of the Cohabitacyon of the Faithful with the Unfaithful* (1555). Matthew knew this book well, reading and annotating his copy, and reusing it in successive sermons. Although they had little success, elsewhere the strategy worked to heal old divisions. Promoting Martin Heton, dean of Winchester, to be the next bishop of Winchester in 1597, his supporters reported that Heton had 'mollified the obdurate hearts of irreligious subjects' through his 'preaching, hospitality and the wise direction of his life'.[28] And hospitality had further benefits too. As we shall see, Tobie and Frances Matthew used hospitality to build up relationships with powerful local figures in northern England. Sometimes this helped to create a community of Protestants who shared the pastoral Puritanism of the Matthews, sometimes it built alliances with the local nobility who, with Matthew, were responsible for governing the North.

Hospitality was a flashpoint for arguments about the influence that wives could exercise through their 'public housekeeping' and social duties of the clergymen. Supporters of clerical marriage argued that wifely involvement could be of great help providing hospitality. Thomas Becon told his readers that 'St Paul joyneth marriage and hospitality' and reported that 'the marriage of priests is no hindrance but rather a furtherance unto hospitality'.[29] Many ministers agreed that wives were crucial in providing hospitality. Long before it was legal in England, concubinage was accepted in much of the Celtic Church, and many prominent Welsh ministers were married and maintained large households. When Thomas Cromwell's commissioners ordered them to put aside their wives, they refused. Petitioning Henry VIII, they complained that getting rid of their wives meant 'giving up hospitality to the utter undoing of such servants and families as we daily keep'. When Elizabeth I later tried to ban clerical wives from cathedral closes and colleges in 1561, Archbishop Matthew Parker (himself married), asked, 'alas, what policy is this to drive hospitality out of cathedral closes?' Matthew Parker's wife, Margaret Harleston, was recognised as an invaluable assistant to the archbishop, helping him with his 'most splendid and noble buildings and feastings . . . neither her will nor industry wanting'.[30]

Supporters of clerical marriage argued that by taking on the household task of hospitality, wives freed up their husbands to do more important things (like preparing sermons). Writing in the early days of Elizabeth's reign, Jean Véron argued that a wife was a great asset to a busy minister. He noted that single men, particularly those who 'keep hospitality', were forever being bothered by servants who wanted help solving minor domestic crises. In contrast, Véron imagined a wife handling all domestic matters, leaving her husband free to concentrate on his work. If a minister chose a 'trusty yokefellow', Véron wrote, then 'he need not trouble himself with all, but [can] give himself quietly to his own book'.[31] Elizabeth Gouge, married to the noted godly preacher, William Gouge, did just this. At her funeral, it was noted that Elizabeth had 'providently ordered the affairs of her house, whereby he [William] had the more leisure to attend to his public function'.[32]

It was generally assumed that women were more suited to the domestic sphere than their husbands. While William Perkins presented hospitality as the duty of 'the Master of the family', he accepted that women were central to its success, noting that the prophet Elisha received hospitality from the 'woman of Shunam' as well as her husband. Buying and cooking food were thought to come under the wife's aegis, with menus to be planned, shopping to be done and servants to supervise. Perkins recognised that in the matter of feeding the family, women were usually in charge, advising husbands against 'challenging' or 'prescribing' their wives 'in all matters domestical, but in some to leave her to her own will and judgement'.[33] In the *English Housewife* (1615), Gervase

Markham thought that women would be responsible for preparing and serving food for entertainments ranging from 'great feasts' to 'an ordinary proportion, which any good man may keep in his family for the entertainment of his true and worthy friends'.[34]

Wives could improve the hospitality on offer through clever household management, with the ability to economise being highly praised. These skills were not only practical, but had a biblical pedigree. Good husbandry (or as the puritan writers John Dodd and Robert Cleaver renamed it, 'good housewifery') was a feminine virtue promoted in the Bible and therefore suitable for clerical wives. In their household manual, Dodd and Cleaver argued that 'St Paul would have a woman a good home-keeper', and told their readers to emulate 'the good husbandry which the spirit of God teacheth'.[35] Furthermore, it had practical benefits too. William Harrison believed that uxorious housekeeping had definitely improved the quality and extent of clerical hospitality in Elizabethan England. Wives were better at keeping households and at economising: 'their meat and drink is more orderly and frugally dressed', Harrison wrote, and 'their furniture of household is more convenient and better looked to'. Harrison, a married priest, had firsthand experience of this household management.[36] Successive writers praised clerical wives for helping their husbands to provide hospitality in the most trying of circumstances. Caleb Dalechamp recalled that when Peter Martyr fled Italy, he 'left his great riches and preferments' behind for a small income in Strasbourg. Thanks to the skilful economizing of Martyr's wife, however, Dalechamp reported that couple were still able to be 'bountiful to the poor and needy'.[37] Nicholas Guy praised Elizabeth Gouge's housekeeping skills and frugality at her funeral, noting that she learned 'piety, modesty [and] good housewifery' in the minister's household where she grew up. When the chancellor of York, Phineas Hodson, erected a monument to his wife, Jane, in 1636, he praised his wife's household economy. Jane had given birth to twenty-four children by her death at thirty-eight (her husband noted she was '*mater foecunda*') so her astute financial management was perhaps particularly important.[38]

Wifely involvement in the household economy of clerics was, however, a contentious topic. As well as concerns that wives were 'over reaching' their sphere of influence, there was a widespread fear that by administering household finances, clerical wives were depriving congregations of the charity they needed. The draft bill of 1575 contained complaints that money intended for hospitality was now being used to support clerical families, raising important questions about how far clerical income – and therefore the clerical household – was part of a public sphere or a private family home.[39] It was a common trope that married clerics did not provide hospitality. John Harington paid William Overton, bishop of Coventry, a backhanded compliment when he claimed that Overton 'keepeth good hospitality for the poor, which I have seldom heard a married bishop commended for'.[40] When William Cecil worried about the lack of clerical hospitality in 1585, he was sure that it was caused by the wives and families of ministers. He wrote that the 'bishops and clergy' who should be providing hospitality were instead: 'covetous, [e]specially such as have wives and children'. Cecil blamed clerical poverty – used by ministers to justify poor hospitality – on the recent practice of clergy making 'alienations of their liberties for their children'.[41] There was some truth to the complaints. When Tobie Matthew arrived in Durham in 1583, he found that over £3500 of leases had been misappropriated by the cathedral canons, who used funds intended for alms and hospitality to bolster prebendal incomes. Matthew was forced into a long and ultimately unsuccessful legal battle to try and get lands back from Katherine Whittingham, the widow of a former dean of Durham, William Whittingham.[42]

The thorny question of income and property reflected arguments about how far wives controlled the clerical household or its purse strings. It is significant that the 1575 bill which criticised senior clerics for spending money on their families, also ordered women to withdraw from 'the order, rule or government of the household'. Discussions about hospitality – an activity that offered wives the greatest potential to discharge her husband's clerical duties – highlighted this disquiet. This raised the larger question of how clerical wives should behave. Should the ideal wife model herself on the biblical Mary of Bethany – devoted to a quiet and private piety that could be emulated by any godly laywoman? Or instead, should she aim to be like Martha, taking advantage of the special status that her marriage gave her and maintaining a household open to all?

The earliest depictions of clerical wives ignored any special status conferred on to them through marriage, and instead promoted them as a model of female piety that could be emulated by anyone. Asked to preach at the wedding of a minister in 1625, Thomas Taylor found inspiration for his sermon in the biblical story of Elizabeth, mother of St John the Baptist and wife of a priest, Zachariah. Taylor told the bride: 'Elizabeth, a priest's wife, [was] yet commended by the Spirit of God for a holy and just woman', so 'therefore the wives of Ministers are set by God in the foremost ranks of Christ, holy, gracious and godly women'. Even though Taylor had chosen the story of Elizabeth *because* she was married to a priest (like the bride in front of him), Taylor ignored the exceptional position that Elizabeth's marriage had placed her in. Rather than dwell on any special duties offered by clerical marriage, Taylor presented the ideal clerical wife as the perfect embodiment of female piety: 'it was expected that Elizabeth should shine in grace and godliness above ordinary women, because she was Zachary's wife, the priest's wife'.[43] It was an increasingly common trope that the clerical household was a model for others to follow. Richard Bernard, a Puritan minister, warned readers of his clerical handbook that he had learned by experience that: 'common people respect more a good teacher's life, than his learning, and reverence the person and not his preaching so much.' Preaching at a clerical synod in York, Archbishop Tobie Matthew warned ministers to conduct their home lives according to the ideals they set out in the pulpit, telling them: 'a minister in the Church is as a light set upon a candlestick which if it burns clearly men do with comfort behold it, if it burn duskishly with smoke and stench, they that are in the house cannot but perceive it'.[44]

This was a vision of female piety that was private and inward-looking. Advice manuals for the laity, many of them written by married clergymen, imagined the ideal wife occupied with private devotions and the religious observances of children and servants. John Dodd (married to the daughter of a clergyman) and Robert Cleaver thought that wives could be a 'fellow-helper' of their husbands, but only 'indoors, touching godliness'. Writing in 1612, Richard Bernard imagined a wife as her 'husband's shadow', representing his religious ideals 'as the moon doth from the sun'. Mothers had a particular duty to bring up their children religiously as 'the first that instructs the child'. It was a pattern echoed in *The Householder's Help for Domesticall Discipline*, where the author noted that in the Book of Proverbs 'Soloman presupposeth that all godly mothers will be helpers to their husbands in the religious and godly instruction of their children'.[45] This internal domestic piety was echoed in biographies of women in clerical households. Elizabeth Joceline – who learned the 'studies of piety' in the household of her grandfather, Bishop Chaderton – stressed the importance of private female devotions in a letter she wrote to her unborn child, published as *The Mother's Legacie*. Elizabeth Gouge, married to the Puritan preacher William Gouge, reportedly devoted herself to the religious instruction of the household, including teaching her children Gouge's catechism. When she engaged in charitable works, she did so outside the household – rather than the traditional model of providing charity through hospitality at home.[46]

Ministers explored the potential conflict between the public functions of the clerical household and the private duties of the wife through the story of Martha and Mary. Writers usually praised Mary, the sister who sat quietly at Jesus's feet, rather than Martha, who rushed around providing hospitality. In his book on household 'oeconomy', William Perkins contrasted the two sisters, praising Mary's behaviour as 'commendable'. The Puritan minister, Stephen Geree, praised Elizabeth Machell as the ideal of a godly gentlewoman in his sermon at her funeral in 1639. 'Whereas other women trouble themselves with many things like Martha', he told his congregation, Elizabeth Machell 'set her soul upon that one thing necessary, choosing with Mary that better part that could not be taken from her'. And what was appropriate for godly women was also appropriate for the wives of ministers. Preaching at the marriage of a minister in 1625, Thomas Taylor used the story of Mary and Martha to encourage private female devotions. He told the newly married clerical wife that 'it is the woman who feareth the Lord that shall be praised', and that 'if Christ commend a woman, it shall not be Martha for her good husbandry, but Mary for choosing the better part'.[47]

There was, however, evidence that despite the praise heaped on them for private devotions, plenty of clerical wives were actively involved in their husband's household. Occasionally authors admitted that some wives were more inspired by Martha. When Nicholas Guy preached at the funeral of Elizabeth Gouge in 1625, he argued that Martha, not Mary, was the model of appropriate religiosity. While Mary 'washed Christ's feet with her tears, and dried them with her hair', Martha was far more practical. Guy noted that Martha welcomed Jesus warmly, and likened Elizabeth Gouge to Martha, telling his congregation that there were: 'few such Marthas who meet Christ coming towards them, we rather flee from him'.[48] The Gouges' marriage highlight some of the tensions about roles within marriage, and indeed the disparity between what ministers might preach and their experiences. At Blackfriars, William Gouge famously preached a series of sermons justifying female submission in marriage that were so unpopular with women in the congregation he was forced to explain himself. Later, he argued that he actually envisioned (or maybe just experienced) a household where the wife was 'a joint governor of the family', and in which the husband would 'refer the ordering of many things to her discretion'.[49]

Many clerical wives saw themselves as playing an active part in their husbands' ministry. Joyce Featley felt able to advise two of the most well-known London preachers – her husband Daniel Featley and Thomas Gataker – on what they should be preaching about.[50] The household, however, was where women could discharge their husbands' pastoral duties. Anne Thompson has shown that ministers frequently relied on their wives – or rather widows – to distribute alms after their death, illustrating the extent to which clerical wives already had a charitable role within the community. The pattern was replicated by the wives of bishops and archdeacons, who were also often responsible for distributing charitable bequests. Thomas Becon imagined exactly this sort of role for clerical wives, hoping that they would do work that was profitable to the 'commonwealth'. Sometimes this was informal, with wives acting as intermediaries between their husbands and parishioners. Parishioners could confide things to a minister's wife they might not be able to say to his face, and of course, clerical wives were welcomed to a birthing chamber where men were not. It is clear that in these situations the minister's wife was regarded as having a special status, bestowed on her by marriage. Sometimes, however, clerical wives overstepped the mark, taking on more of their husbands' responsibilities than was thought appropriate. There are accounts of clerical wives baptising children and even taking services on their husband's behalf.[51] More usual however, was the 'public housekeeping' – most notably hospitality – when clerical wives were responsible for some of their husbands' professional duties.

Contemporary recognition of this special status was, however, muted. Although some memorials and monuments to clerical wives celebrated their commitment to hospitality, it was not the norm. After her death in 1617, Elizabeth Rogers – married to the archdeacon of Chester – was celebrated for her 'love to her husband and children, liberalities to the poor' and her 'bountiful hospitality'.[52] It was, however, fairly unusual to mention hospitality, even among those women who were renowned for helping their husbands entertain and feed the poor. The memorial to Frances Matthew celebrated her private 'virtues. . . above her sex', namely her 'beauty', 'piety' and 'wisdom'. It made no mention of the hospitality she had provided with Tobie Matthew over the previous decades. Instead, hospitality was portrayed as part of the professional duties of a cleric, recorded on the nearby tomb of Tobie Matthew. There the inscription noted that the archbishop's 'singular hospitality should be recorded: his house was a perpetual source of entertainment for the rich and charity for the poor'.[53] The same distinction was true for Cecily Sandys, another widow of an archbishop of York famed for his hospitality. Her memorial concentrated on her influence within the family: she 'carefully educated' her children with Archbishop Sandys; 'wisely governed his family'; and 'charitably relieved the poor'. She was, as the memorial concluded, 'a true mirror of a Christian matron'.[54] While memorials to Elizabethan and Stuart clerical widows recognized the status given to them by marriage, these wives were portrayed as an example of private domestic piety that could be emulated by anyone. Cecilia Freake, for example, was recorded on her memorial as being the 'relict' of Edmund Freake, successively bishop of Rochester, Norwich and Worcester. Her qualities however, were limited to being a 'good wife, and a pious widow'.[55] Memorials were some of the earliest attempts to describe what it meant to be a clergyman's wife, and these often reflected the uneasy line that clerical wives trod between personal piety and the requirements of the professional clergyman's household.

Frances Matthew was responsible for several of these memorials, erecting monuments to her mother, sisters and brothers-in-law, all of which celebrated the place of women (in particular the Barlow sisters) in the English Reformation. Frances's own experiences demonstrate the influence that clerical marriage could offer Evangelical women. However, the memorials that she commissioned also demonstrate a continuing uneasiness about celebrating the unique opportunities provided to clerical wives.

Frances Matthew was well known for her commitment to Protestantism. Her son described her as 'much more fervent towards the Puritanical sole-Scripture way' than Archbishop Tobie Matthew, and complained that she was always 'as busy with Scripture as if it had been some glove upon her fingers' ends'. Frances's reputation for godliness was well known and her son noted that 'she was held in a mighty opinion' by Puritans, lay and clerical.[56] Frances had an impeccable pedigree as a Protestant reformer. Her parents married in the reign of Henry VIII, long before it was legal, and then were forced into exile. After Elizabeth's succession, William Barlow was made bishop of Chichester, moving his wife and seven children into the episcopal palace. During the first decades of Elizabeth's reign, all five of the Barlow daughters married clerics, and it appears that their choices reflect a genuine commitment to

Evangelical reform. Frances was embedded in a network of godly clerics, cementing relationships with Protestant allies through marriage and the connections offered by standing as a godparent. When Frances's first son, Matthew Parker, was born in 1575, his godparents included her brother-in-law, William Day, the future bishop of Winchester. A few years later when, Frances gave birth to another son, John, at Christ Church in Oxford, she chose her sister Anne – married to Herbert Westphaling – to be a godmother, while Laurence Humphrey was one of John's godfathers. Frances later asked Laurence Humphrey's wife, Joan Inkforby – a former Marian exile – to be godmother to her 'most dearly beloved son', Samuel. And many of Frances's own godchildren were clerical offspring, mostly the sons and daughters of bishops.[57]

Frances Matthew was keenly aware of her inheritance as a child of one of the first Evangelical clerics and was eager to highlight the Barlow family's place in the Protestant hierarchy. In 1595, a family tree was drawn up for Frances Matthew listing all her parents' children – seven of whom survived into adulthood. All the daughters married clergymen, and by 1595 – when Frances commissioned the family tree – all five were married to bishops. In 1598, Frances once more stressed the Barlow legacy when she commissioned a memorial for her sister, Anthonine, whom she described as a 'daughter to Bishop Barlow and wife to Bishop Whickham . . . two brethren of good name and place'. The memorial then noted that all of Anthonine's sisters were married to bishops. Frances once again highlighted the Barlows' influence in a memorial to another sister, Elizabeth Day, which noted that not only was Elizabeth married to a bishop, but that all her brothers-in-law were bishops. And these same facts – an episcopal father, an archbishop as a husband, and bishops as brothers-in-law – were repeated on Frances Matthew's own memorial in York Minster.[58] The familial connections, the marriages and the friendships developed in these clerical households shaped the Church of England, and Frances was keen that her family's contribution was recognised.

While the Barlow memorials celebrated these clerical matches, they were silent on the benefits that clerical marriage offered the women, perhaps reflecting a continuing unease about the influence of clerical wives. However, Frances was an important part of the households that Tobie Matthew oversaw in Oxford, Durham and York. He appointed her sole executor of his will: 'relying with all confidence upon her care and providence (of which I have had good experience for the space of almost fifty years).'[59] She had extensive experience of clerical households when she married Tobie Matthew in 1577, bringing with her the knowledge of the influence that episcopal wives could exercise. In addition to growing up in an episcopal household, Frances's first husband – Matthew Parker – was the son of Archbishop Matthew Parker, and after they married the young couple moved into Lambeth Palace. There Frances encountered Margaret Parker *née* Harleston who was renowned for her hospitality and for the help she gave to the archbishop. Margaret introduced new ordinances to reform the household, and a contemporary biography described her ordering her 'housekeeping so nobly and splendidly . . . that all things answered that venerable dignity'. Frances also experienced less prominent clerical households too. After Matthew Parker's death, she lived with her sister, Elizabeth Day, and her husband, William, in Eton College.[60]

The Matthews offered hospitality and accommodation to godly clerics, replicating the informal household seminaries which Tom Webster has identified as being so important in the emergence of Puritanism in the 1630s. An episcopal income offered a great deal of potential for patronage and support. One minister, John Favour, prepared large chunks of his history of the Church while staying in the Matthews' household, recalling energetic discussions with Tobie Matthew over breakfast. Another godly minister and author, Edmund Bunny, had his own rooms in the archiepiscopal palace in Cawood, dying there in 1618.[61] Frances was sometimes responsible for initiating these relationships. Despite Tobie Matthew's reservations, Frances sent their son Samuel to study at Peterhouse in Cambridge under the guidance of Samuel Ward, and following her son's death, Frances continued to maintain close connections with Cambridge and Ward. It was Frances who asked Ward to find a godly tutor – Richard Garbutt – to live with and tutor her grandson, Josias. Garbutt was so taken with the community of northern Puritans he met while with the Matthews that he decided to stay in Yorkshire. Frances also appears to have been behind the choice of John Scott to be the new dean of York Minster in 1624. Though Scott was a disastrous choice – he was imprisoned for his gambling debts – the appointment brought his wife Dorothy Scott (Frances's niece and goddaughter) and their children to live in the Minster Close. Dorothy shared a godly outlook with Frances and other clerical wives in the Minster Close, despite the growing enthusiasm for Laudianism among some of the Minster's clerics. Along with another prebendal wife, Jane Hodson, Dorothy secretly hosted a Puritan conventicle in the deanery until it was discovered in 1627.[62]

Frances was also a bridge between Tobie Matthew and the laity, providing hospitality that established powerful alliances and making friendships that sustained those connections. A recipe book compiled in the 1620s and 1630s by a local minister and York prebendary, Henry Fairfax, illustrates the networks of 'soft power' threaded through the northern Church. Fairfax, himself brother of the local nobleman, Ferdinando Fairfax, married local gentlewoman, Mary Cholmley, in 1627. The recipe book that Henry and Mary compiled after their marriage included several recipes passed on to them by Frances Matthew – some of which, in turn, had been passed on to her by noblewomen. One, a recipe for liquorice juice, had come to Frances from Lady Bowes – married to a major landowner in Durham who was a key supporter of the Elizabethan regime. Another, for liquorice tablets, was designed to be used for either illness or for an after-dinner sweet, reflecting the extent of Frances Matthew's frequent entertaining.[63]

The entertaining that Frances and Matthew did at their palaces in York and Durham was politically sensitive, and a key part of Matthew's government. As well as hosting friends, the Matthews were expecting to win over enemies. Richard Bernard, a Puritan cleric and former Separatist, dedicated one of his books to 'the chief officers, gentlemen, domesticall attendants and the rest of the family' of Archbishop Tobie Matthew. 'You are in an eminent place', Bernard told them: 'no way can you so glorify God as by practical profession, nor advance before the enemy the honour of the Most Revd your Lord and Master more, than by a holy conversation'.[64] Frances developed friendships that underpinned Tobie Matthew's political alliances, using her household and hospitality. One such friendship was her relationship with Anne, wife of Francis Clifford, the earl of Cumberland and the most eminent nobleman in the north. The Cliffords visited the Matthews at Bishopthorpe palace, and when Lady Anne Clifford was in York the following month, Frances Matthew went to see her along with Lord Sheffield's daughters. They were clearly close, as Anne Clifford recorded in her diary that 'this night' Frances Matthew 'lay with me'.[65] In addition, Frances established her household as a centre of godly domesticity in imitation of local noble households, like that of the Earl and Countess of Huntingdon at York in the 1580s and 1590s. As one contemporary noted, northerners who had 'a desire to bestow good breeding upon their daughters thought themselves happy, and that they had more than half bred their daughters, if they could get them entertained into Mrs Matthew's service'.[66]

Sometimes there was a chasm between the ideal of the harmonious clerical household and the reality, and Tobie and Frances Matthew's marriage was far from serene. Frances complained bitterly about moving north, and indeed was slow to follow her husband to Durham, choosing to stay near family in Oxford instead. There is also evidence that while in Durham, Tobie Matthew had an extramarital affair with his chaplain's wife (possibly fathering at least one child with her). Frances sourly called her a 'hot arsed Queen', and the news blackened Matthew's reputation at court: Lady Elizabeth Russell complained to her nephew, Robert Cecil, that Matthew was not an 'upright' man.[67] Although the injunctions of 1559 focused on scandalous wives, husbands were as likely to stray and their sexual activities could be as damaging to the reputation of the clergy. Archbishop Edwin Sandys found his reputation damaged after he was reportedly found in bed with an inn-keeper's wife. Sandys claimed this was an attempt to smear his reputation, and certainly it became a high profile case, eventually making it to the Star Chamber. Although Sandys was exonerated, the whiff of sexual impropriety hung around for the rest of his career. And bishops weren't the only clergy to struggle with their marriages: violence, drunkenness, defamation and adultery afflicted clerical marriages like those of their lay counterparts.[68]

John Harington described Frances Matthew as 'the best reported and reputed of her sort I think in England'.[69] Throughout the period, Frances enjoyed a favourable reputation in lay and clerical circles. She excelled at the expected wifely skills and yet also had an influence that extended beyond Archbishop Matthew's household. She communicated with leading clerics like Samuel Ward, and local ministers including Francis Bunny dedicated books to her. Her monument likened her to the Queen of Carthage, noting the 'rare example' of her learning, and praising her donation of books to York Minster. Her gift brought widespread public benefits: 'first derived upon this Church, and through it flowing upon the country'. Here was a woman actively shaping the post-Reformation Church.[70]

Yet, wifely involvement was not always appreciated by contemporaries who criticised overly-powerful wives and mocked their clerical husbands. In 1575, Richard Cox's wife was widely blamed for the bishop's refusal to hand over leases to the Queen, with Roger North warning him: 'let not your wife's shallow experience carry you too far, least she lay your honour and credit aground and haply make a shipwreck of the whole'.[71] Bishop Edmund Freake was said to be afraid of his wife, claiming he had to do what she wanted or 'she would make him weary of life'. And indeed, Eric Carlson suggests that the 1575 bill restricting wifely involvement in the clerical household may have been a response to the efforts of Cecily Freake.[72]

Despite ambiguity about the status and influence of clerical wives, it is evident that the public housekeeping required of early modern clerics offered an opportunity for their wives to have an impact. Hospitality was an important duty of the clergy, from parish priests to archbishops and as it was delivered from the household, it was also an area where clerical wives could – and did – exercise considerable influence. Contemporaries recognised this, and the arguments about clerical hospitality in this period were driven by criticisms of how far women were discharging their husbands' professional duties. The examples here illustrate how marriage offered an opportunity for Evangelical women to engage in the Reformation process, working alongside their husbands. The role that women could play in the household and the relationship between the clerical family and the wider community were fraught and often uneasy. Clerical wives, and increasingly clerical families, were held up as models of piety that the laity could emulate and as many of the memorials to the earliest clergy wives demonstrate, at times it appears that there was a concerted effort to ignore any special influence offered by marriage to ministers. However, as historians have shown, clerical wives were recognised as occupying a special status in early modern society seen in numerous interactions at parish level and beyond. Clerical wives, themselves, appear to have embraced these opportunities with women like Frances Matthew using the resources of the clerical household – and the hospitality that was expected – to pursue her own commitment to godly reform.

The lives of these women illustrate the powerful, yet often hidden, networks underpinning the Elizabethan and Jacobean Church. As Weisner-Hanks argues, it is imperative to trace the influence of individual clerical wives outside of the 'private sphere' to understand the complexities of the Reformation process.[73] Although clerical wives may have been encouraged to emulate Mary of Bethany, it is evident that many instead chose to follow in the path of Martha, using their household as a tool of the Reformation.

## Notes

1 National Archives, Kew (hereafter NA), 'An act concerning good hospitality among the clergy', State Papers (hereafter SP) 15/24/8 ff. 21–5.

2 Helen Parish, *Clerical Marriage and the English Reformation* (2000) pp. 227–8. Helen Parish, '"It was Never Good World Sence Minister Must Have Wyves": Clerical Marriage and Anti-Clericalism in Reformation England, *Journal of Religious History*, vol 36 no 1 (2012), pp. 52–69. Eric Carlson, 'Clerical Marriage and the English Reformation', *Journal of British Studies*, vol 13 no 1 (1992) pp. 1–31.

3 Discussions about continental Protestantism include P. Matheson, 'A reformation for women: sin, grace and gender in Argula Von Grumbach', *Scottish Journal of Theology*, vol 49, (1996), pp. 1–17. Marjorie Elizabeth Plummer, 'Partner in His Calamities: Pastors Wives, Married Nuns and the Experience of Clerical Marriage in the Early German Reformation', *Gender and History*, vol 20 no 2 (2008), pp. 207–27.

4 Sara Mendelson and Patricia Crawford, *Women in Early Modern England 1550–1720* (Oxford, 1998), pp. 30–1. Merry Weisner-Hanks, 'Women and the Reformations: Reflections on Recent Research', *History Compass*, vol 2 no 1 (2004), pp. 1–27.

5 Mary Prior, 'Reviled and Crucified marriages: the position of Tudor Bishop's wives' in *Women in English Society 1500–1800* ed. Mary Prior (London, 1985), pp. 118–48. Rosamund Oates, *Moderate Radical: Tobie Matthew and the English Reformation* (Oxford, 2019).

6 Felicity Heal: *Of Prelates and Princes: A Study of the Economic and Social Position of the Tudor Episcopate* (Cambridge, 1980). Kenneth Fincham, *Prelate as Pastor: The Episcopate of James I* (Oxford, 1990).

7 Luke 10: 38–42. John 11: 1–33.

8 Anne Thompson, *Parish Clergy Wives in Elizabethan England* (Leiden, 2019), pp. 72–86. Parish, 'Clerical Marriage and Anti-Clericalism', *Journal of Religious History*, pp. 52–69.

9 Heinrich Bullinger, *Der Christlich Eestand* (Zurich, 1540). Heinrich Bullinger, *The Christen State of Matrimonye* (trans.) Miles Coverdale (Antwerp, 1541), sig. D7r. John Ponet *An Apologie Fully Answering . . . Thomas Martin . . . against the godly marriage of priestes* (Strasbourg, 1556) sigs. A2r, B8v. Tobie Matthew's copy is in York Minster Library (YML) shelfmark V/2.J.16 (1).

10 William Perkins, *Christian Oeconomie* (London, 1609), p. 66. *Articles to be Enquired of from the Diocesean Visitation of Tobie Matthew* (London, 1623), p. 17.

11 Bullinger, *Christen State of Matrimonye*, sig. D7v. Carrie Euler, 'Heinrich Bullinger, Marriage, and the English Reformation: "The Christen State of Matrimonye" in England, 1540–53', *The Sixteenth Century Journal*, vol 34 no 2, (2003), pp. 367–93.

12 Ponet, *An Apologie*, sig. I 5r–v, I 8 r. Matthew Parker (ed.), *A Defence of Priests' Marriage* (1567) pp. 32, 42, 156. 1 Timothy 3: 2–12.

13 John Favour, *Antiquity Triumphing Over Novelty* (London, 1619) sig. A3r.

14 Easton Church Winchester, many thanks to Professor Claire Cross for the transcription. Peter Sherlock, 'Monuments, Reputation, and Clerical Marriage in Reformation England: Bishop Barlow's Daughters', *Gender and History*, vol 16 no 1 (2004), pp. 60–4.

15 R. Basch 'The Changing Status and Identity of English Bishops' Wives, *c.* 1549–1625' University of London PhD thesis, 2016, pp. 83–7.

16 N. Guy, *Pieties Pillar: A Sermon Preached at the Funeral of Mistress Elizabeth Gouge* (London, 1626), p. 41.

17 Prior, 'Reviled and Crucified', p. 121. Susan Karant-Nunn, 'The Emergence of the Pastoral Family in the German Reformation: The Parsonage as a site of socio-religious change', in C. Dixon and Luise Schorn-Schütte (ed.), *The Protestant Clergy of Early Modern Europe* (London, 2003), pp. 79–99.

18 Caleb Dalechamp, *Christian Hospitality* (London, 1632), p. 50

19 W. Harrison, 'The Description of England' in Ralph Holinshed, *Chronicles of England, Scotlande and Irelande* (London, 1577), sig. 94v. Felicity Heal *Hospitality in Early Modern England* (Oxford, 1990), pp. 259–72.

20 Dean and Chapter MS, Durham Cathedral (hereafter DCD) 'York Book' T/YB fos. 50–2. British Library (hereafter BL), 'Matthew Parker to William Cecil', Lansdowne (hereafter Lans) MS 7 fo. 153. NA Memorandum by Burghley' SP 12/184/50, fo. 136r.

21 BL Tobie Matthew to William Cecil' Lans MS36 ff. 124, 126.

22 DCD/T/YB ff. 31. BL Lans MS 36 fo. 126. Oates, *Moderate Radical*, pp. 109–14.

23 *Cal MS Sal.* vol 14, Proclamation Against Engrossing and Transporting of Wheat', p. 294. Ilana Krausman Ben-Amos, 'Gifts and Favors: Informal support in Early Modern England', *The Journal of Modern History*, vol 72, no 2 (2000), pp. 295–338. Steve Hindle, 'Dearth, Fasting and Alms: The Campaign for General Hospitality in Late Elizabethan England' *Past and Present*, vol 172 (2001), pp. 44–86

24 *Three Sermons or Homilies to Move Compassion Towards the Poor and Needy* (London, 1596), sig. B2r. quoting Isaiah 58: 6–7. NA 'William James to William Cecil', SP 12/263/55 fo. 74. NA 'Decay of the Borders' SP 15/33/1 fo. 1. Thompson, *Parish Clergy Wives*, p. 193.

25 *Calendar of the Manuscripts of the Most Honourable the Marquess of Salisbury . . . preserved at Harfield House* (hereafter Cal. MS Sal.) (London, 1883–1976), 'Tobie Matthew to William Cecil', vol 7, pp. 451–3; 'Copy of Ecclesiastical Bill' vol. 8, p. 34.

26 Alan Macfarlane (ed.), *The Diary of Ralph Josselin, 1616–1683* (London, 1976), p. 185. Joan Thirsk, *Food In Early Modern England: Phases, Fads, Fashions 1500–1760* (London, 2007) pp. 97–9.

27 Caleb Dalechamp, *Christian Hospitality* (London, 1632), pp. 6, 7, 10.

28 NA SP 12/ 263/55 fo. 74. *Cal MS. Sal.* 'William Sandys & co. to Robert Devereux', vol. 14, p. 11. Peter Martyr Vermigli, *Treatise of the Cohabitacyon of the Faithful with the Unfaithful* (Strasbourg, 1555), York Minster Library, V/2.K.1. Alexandra Walsham, 'Supping with Satan's Disciples: Spiritual and Secular Sociability in Post-Reformation England', in Adam Morton and Nadine Lewycky (eds), *Getting Along: Religious Identities and Confessional Relations in Early Modern England* (Farnham, 2012), p. 45.

29 Thomas Becon, 'The Boke of Matrimony', in Thomas Becon, *Collected Works* (John Day, London, 1564), sig. 614r.

30 For example Robert ap Rhys and Hywel ap Dai, Glanmore Williams, *Renewal and Reformation, Wales c. 1415–1642* (Oxford, 1987), p. 131. Heal, *Hospitality* p. 252. John Strype, *The Life and Acts of Matthew Parker* (Oxford, 1821), vol 3 p. 51, vol 12 p. 27.

31 Jean Véron, *A Strong Defence of the Marriage of Priests* (London, n.d. 1563?), sig. B3r.

32 Guy, *Pieties Pillar*, p. 44

33 Perkins, *Christian Oeconomie*, pp. 126–7, 171.

34 G. Markham, *The English Housewife* (ed.) Michael R Best (London & Buffalo, 1994), pp. 121–4

35 John Dodd and Robert Cleaver, *A Godly Form of Household Government* (London, 1598), pp. 68, 90, 95

36 W. Harrison, *The Description of England*, ed. Georges Edelen (Folger Library, Washington, 1967), p. 37.

37 Dalechamp, *Christian Hospitality*, p. 50.

38 Guy, *Pieties Pillar*, p. 44. Drake, *Eboracum*, vol 2 p. 508. 'foelix oecomoama'.

39 NA SP 15/24/8 fos. 21–5.

40 John Harington, *Nugae Antiquae* (London, 1804) vol 2, pp. 117–18.

41 NA SP 12/184/50, fo. 136r.

42 BL 'Tobie Matthew to William Cecil' Lans MS 39 fo. 24. DCD/T/YB ff. 2r-11v, 19v–31v.

43 T. Taylor, *A Good Husband and a Good Wife* (London, 1625), pp. 6, 26.

44 Bodleian Library, Oxford, (hereafter Bod.), 'Sermon Notebook', Additional MS, A 89 fo. 155r–v. Richard Bernard, *The Faithful Shepherd* (London, 1607 edn), p. 10. Alexandra Walsham, 'Holy Families: The Spiritualisation of the Early Modern Household Revisited', *Studies in Church History* (2014), pp. 122–60.

45 Dodd and Cleaver, *A Godly Form of Household Government*, pp. 60–1. Richard Bernard, *Joshua's Godly Resolution* (London, 1612), pp. 32–3. R. R. *The Householders Help for Domestical Discipline* (London, 1615), sig. A2v.

46 Guy, *Pieties Pillar*, p. 44–7. Elizabeth Joceline, *The Mother's Legacie to her Unborn Child* (London, 1632), sig. A5.

47 Perkins, *Christian Oeconomie*, p. 167. Taylor, *A Good Husband*, p. 5. Stephen Geree, 'To the Truly Noble and Pious Sisters', *The Ornament of Women* (London, 1639) sig. a3v.

48 Guy, *Pieties Pillar*, pp. 2–6.

49 William Gouge, *Of Domesticall Duties* (London, 1622), sig., *3v-4*, pp. 269–73.

50 Thomas Gataker cited in Eric Carlson, 'Funeral Sermons as Sources: The Example of Female Piety in Pre-1640 Sermons', *Albion*, vol 32, no 4 (2000), p. 586

51 Thompson, *Parish Clergy Wives*, pp. 132–5. Michelle Wolfe, 'The Tribe of Levi: Gender, Family and Vocation in English Clerical Households, *c*. 1590–1714', Ohio State University PhD thesis, 2004, p. 45.

52 Peter Sherlock, *Monuments and Memory in Early Modern England* (Farnham, 2008), chapter 4.

53 The original monumental brass was destroyed in a nineteenth-century fire, but an inscription can be found (along with a translation) in Francis Drake, *Eboracum* (York, 1788), vol 2, pp. 342–4, 512.

54 Memorial on the north wall of the chancel in St Mary's, Woodham Ferrers, Essex, erected in 1619.

55 Basch, 'English Bishops' Wives', p. 183.

56 T. Matthew, *A True historical relation of the Conversion of Sir Tobie Matthew* ed. A. H. Mathew (London, 1904), p. 131.

57 YML, Frances Matthew, 'A note of all my children', Add MS 322. Borthwick Institute for Archives, (hereafter BIA) York, Probate Register 40, ff., 397r–398v. Oates, *Moderate Radical*, pp. 59–60.

58 Oates, *Moderate Radical*, pp. 175–7. Sherlock, 'Monuments, Reputations and Clerical Marriage', pp. 57–82

59 BIA Probate Register 40 fo. 195r.

60 YML Add MS 322. Basch, 'English Bishops' Wives', p. 117.

61 W. Sheils, 'Bunny, Edmund (1540–1618)', *Oxford Dictionary of National Biography* (2004). Favour, *Antiquity Triumphing* Novelty, preface. Tom Webster, *Godly Clergy in Early Stuart England: The Caroline Puritan Movement* c. *1620–1643* (Cambridge, Cambridge, 1997), ch. 1.

62 Oates, *Moderate Radical*, pp. 232, 237.

63 *Ibid.*, p. 106. George Weddell, *Arcana Fairfaxiana Manuscripta* (Newcastle-Upon-Tyne, 1890), pp. 140, 145–6.

64 Richard Bernard, *The Sinner's Safetie* (London, 1609), dedicatory epistle.

65 YML 'Tobie Matthew's Preaching Diary' Add MS 18 pp. 115–17. D. J. H. Clifford (ed.), *The Diaries of Lady Anne Clifford* (Stroud, 2003), p. 44

66 Durham University Library, Mickelton and Spearman MS 23 fo. 125r. Claire Cross, *The Puritan Earl: The Life of Henry Hastings, Third Earl of Huntingdon 1536–95* (MacMillan, London, 1966).

67 Oates, *Moderate Radical*, pp. 101–2.

68 Carlson, 'Clerical Marriage', pp. 18, Thompson, *Parish Clergy Wives*, pp. 146–51. Sarah Bastow, 'An Abortive Attempt to Defend an Episcopal Reputation: The Case of Archbishop Edwin Sandys and the Innkeeper's Wife', *History*, vol 97 (2012), pp. 380–401.

69 Harington *Nugae Antiquae*, p. 265.

70 Bod. 'Letter from Samuel Ward to Frances Matthew', Tanner MS 76, fos. 130–1. Francis Bunny, *An Exposition on the Lords Prayer* (London, 1602). Francis Drake, *Eboracum* (York, 1788), vol 2, p. 344.

71 *Cal MS Sal*. 'Roger North to Richard Cox', vol 2, p. 120.

72 Carlson, 'Clerical marriage', p. 19

73 M. Wiesner-Hanks, 'Beyond Women and the Family: Towards a Gender Analysis of the Reformation' *Sixteenth Century Journal*, vol 18 (1987), pp. 311–21. M. Wiesner-Hanks, 'Women and the Reformation: Reflections on Recent Research', *History Compass* 2 (2004), pp. 1–27.

# FROM DEBATE TO EMULATION: WIVES AND DAUGHTERS IN SEVENTEENTH-CENTURY CLERICAL HOUSEHOLDS

Jacqueline Eales, Canterbury Christ Church University

The Reformation debates about the introduction of clerical marriage and the early history of the institution in England in the sixteenth century have been analysed by Helen Parish and Eric Josef Carlson, and there have also been several studies of bishops' wives, but it is only with the recent publication of Anne Thompson's work on Tudor parish clergy wives that we have learned more about the entirely new social group represented by the clerical family.[1] Thompson observes that, although many sources exist for the reconstruction of the lives of clergy wives, it is difficult to find sources reflecting their own voices in the Tudor period.[2] During the seventeenth century sources written by both wives and daughters are available for the study of the clergy family, but their papers have survived mainly in print and were often edited posthumously for the press by their husbands or other admirers.[3] This essay will be primarily concerned with the ways in which these publications related to wider debates about the clerical family and what they can tell us about the construction of an idealised portrayal of their marriages by the English clergy. While the sixteenth century undoubtedly marked the first phase of the development of clerical marriage, the second phase of consolidation spanned the century from 1620–1720, when some notable clerical dynasties were in the making and individual clergy wives and daughters were promoted as worthy of emulation by other women. It will be argued here that the education women received in clerical households equipped them with an intellectual and religious authority that has so far been insufficiently recognised.

Within this setting the writing of women from clerical families was cast as just one of a range of godly practices demonstrating the respectable standing of these wives and daughters as pious role models. Their

https://doi.org/10.16922/jrhlc.6.2.2

habits of prayer, reading, attendance at divine services, charity, care for feeding and healing the poor, and their education of children and servants also marked them out as exceptionally godly and virtuous. This was a period of reconstruction for the national episcopalian church, which faced demands for reform from its Jacobean puritan wing and suffered abolition during the civil wars. Ultimately, the bishops accepted compromise in the form of toleration after the accession of William III and Mary II in 1688, but these debates found little space in the sources to be examined here. Instead our clerical authors framed the lives of their womenfolk as instructional to English men and women of all persuasions: puritans and conformists, parliamentarians and royalists, episcopalians and presbyterians, alike. Their female relatives were worthy of emulation, because of their participation in a national culture of practical piety rather than in the religious controversies of the day. If, as Bishop Joseph Hall maintained in 1624, the British clergy were '*stupor mundi*', the wonder of the world, then their wives were also the subject of admiration and in an elegy of 1657 John Wallis called Margaret Corbet, wife to a fellow Oxford cleric, 'England's Gemme, Great Britains Iewell'.[4] At her burial in 1669 Mabella Finch, the widow of the royalist courtier Sir John Finch, was described as the 'honour' of Canterbury Cathedral where her father, Charles Fotherby, had been Dean. She was praised by the cathedral prebendary Peter du Moulin for carefully covering her wisdom and goodness with 'the vail of humility and singular modesty'.[5]

As these approbations of Margaret Corbet and Mabella Finch indicate, the funeral sermon and associated godly life became the favoured format in print for the praise of individual clerical wives and daughters, particularly in the second half of the seventeenth century, and we can locate this development within the context of ongoing concerns about the status of clergy families. Clerical marriage had been legalized in England by two statutes passed in rapid succession during Edward VI's reign in 1549 and 1552. Overcoming traditionalist views that ministers should be celibate proved to be a long drawn out process and there is evidence of continued hostility to the newly formed clergy family in some parishes throughout the second half of the sixteenth century and into the early years of James I's reign. The social pretensions of bishops' wives attracted satirical comment, while clergy wives were scorned more generally as 'whores' and their children as 'bastards'.[6] The freedom to marry was one of the key defining characteristics of the Protestant clergy and thus the institution of clerical marriage aroused the venom of both

English and Continental Roman Catholic polemicists. In response, the married clergy made lurid accusations of sexual licentiousness against the Roman Catholic priesthood.

William Whately, minister of the parish of Banbury near Oxford and writer of two conduct books about marriage, argued in 1624 that to deny marriage to any kinds of men would lead them to 'filthinesse and uncleanness, And all viciousnesse'. In a repudiation of clerical celibacy he noted that:

> if the condemning of marriage be from the Devill, the allowing of it is from God, and so have all sorts of men universally a full allowance from God to take the benefit of this estate.[7]

Preaching at the wedding of a clerical colleague in 1625 Thomas Taylor, the rector at Saint Mary Aldermanbury in London, informed the congregation that the Roman Catholic ban on clerical marriage was a 'diabolicall doctrine'. It led Catholic priests to indulge in fornication with whores and concubines, and to sodomy, an 'unnaturall filthinesse not to be named among Saints'.[8] By this date the institution of clerical marriage had largely been accepted in the English parishes, although the Protestant clergy were to remain sensitive to attacks from their Roman Catholic opponents. The legitimacy of the clergy family remained a point of contention and when Robert Harris, the President of Trinity College in Oxford, died in 1658 his children were held up by his cousin the Worcestershire cleric, William Durham, as confuting the slander of 'the papists' about the 'ungraciousness' of the children of the clergy.[9] Thomas Hodges also wrote of the canard that 'the Papists urge against the Marriage of our Clergy, the ill manners and lives of their Children' in his treatise defending clerical marriage published in 1673. In response he cited some of the notable clerical dynasties that had sprung up in the seventeenth century:

> Bishop King, late of Chichester, who was the Son of Bishop King, sometime Bishop of London. Bishop Hall, late of Chester, [who] was the Son of Bishop Hall, Bishop of Norwich, . . . And . . . the late reverend and renowned Bp. of Chester, Bp. Wilkins, his Mother was the Daughter of a Minister, viz. Mr. John Dod.[10]

In 1697 George Stanhope, the future dean of Canterbury, returned to this theme when he preached in St Paul's Cathedral at the annual sermon of the Corporation of the Sons of the Clergy that 'I need not say, how much the Clergy and their Families stand like the common mark for Censure and Detraction'.[11]

If clerical marriage was a contentious issue, then subsequent marriages were also problematic and funeral sermons for the clergy often stressed the good choices that ministers made when remarrying even two or three times. For the popular London preacher, Thomas Gataker, a constant life of study made the decision to marry an act of 'prudence' according to his funeral sermon of 1654. His first wife was a widow with two daughters, for whom he arranged marriages with two fellow clerics. After his first and second wives died in childbirth, he remained for many years a widower before marrying a gentlewoman 'of a good esteem for understanding and piety'. Lastly, he married a citizen's widow with whom he lived comfortably for twenty-four years.[12] The preacher John Howes stated in 1659 that Thomas Ball, a Northamptonshire minister, was blessed in his marriages to three 'Religious, and Vertuous Gentlewomen', all of whom expressed love, agreement, faithfulness and affection to him. Howes cited Proverbs 19:14. 'Honour and Riches are the inheritance of Fathers, but a prudent Wife is from the Lord' to emphasise the qualities of all three of Ball's wives.[13] Over a decade later anxiety about ministers who remarried was countered by Thomas Hodges in his *Treatise of Marriage* when he wrote that marriage after the death of a spouse was as lawful for the clergy as it was for the laity: 'the second Marriage in that case tending as much to the ends of Matrimony (Comfort of life, Propagation, remedy of Lust)'.[14]

One of the earliest references to an exemplary clerical wife is to be found in the dedication of William Whately's marriage sermon *A Bride Bush* to his father-in-law, George Hunt, the rector of Collingbourne Ducis in 1617. Whately thanked Hunt for having 'educated for me and bestowed upon me a most excellent and virtuous wife' and claimed to be able to describe a dutiful wife in his sermon 'finding the full dutie of a wife, in exact completenesse, as mortality could affoord, daily and continually performed unto me in mine owne house' by his wife Martha, whom he had married in 1602.[15] This dedication reappeared in subsequent editions of the sermon in 1619 and 1623, and Whately's praise of his wife points both to the relatively new creation of clerical dynasties through intermarriage and to Martha's upbringing within a clergyman's home. We are familiar with the concept of clerical households as seminaries for boys and young men destined for the ministry, but the function of the post-Reformation clergy family as a focus for female training has been largely overlooked. Yet the education that daughters and other young women received in the setting of the clerical household could endow them with an extraordinary spiritual authority with long-term implications for female education and literacy more broadly, which will be discussed more fully below.

The first extended description of an English clergy wife to be printed can be found in *Pieties Pillar*, the funeral sermon preached in 1625 by Nicholas Guy for Elizabeth the wife of William Gouge, the famed conduct book writer and minister at the London City church of St. Anne's, Blackfriars. By this date the funeral sermon and the associated 'godly life' or spiritual biography were well established genres that were rooted in the late mediaeval tradition of the *ars moriendi*, or instruction on the art of dying, as well as in the growing vogue for life writing.[16] Preaching at funerals had become increasingly common after the Reformation, but few of these sermons were published until the 1620s, when funeral sermons for the gentry, the clergy and their wives became increasingly available in print and grew in popularity throughout the seventeenth century. Conventionally, such sermons were divided into two parts with the first addressing a biblical text that was relevant to the life of the deceased and the second directly addressing their life and religious character. Ralph Houlbrooke has identified 214 printed funeral sermons in England in the first half of the century rising to 534 in the second half.[17] Evidence from wills demonstrates that many more sermons were preached at funerals than were printed and those that were published were generally written by men with contacts to the London press, either because they were based in or near the city or had a track record as an established author. From 1650 Samuel Clarke, the presbyterian minister at Saint Benet Fink, London, emerged as one of the most prolific editors of compilations of godly biographies. In 1662, when he endured ejection from his living because of his refusal to conform to the episcopalian church, he published *A Collection of the Lives of Ten Eminent Divines*, in which he included the spiritual biographies of Margaret Corbet and Elizabeth Wilkinson taken from their funeral sermons. In 1677 Clarke published *A Looking Glass for Good Women to Dress Themselves by: Held Forth in the Life and Death of Mrs Katherine Clarke*, a godly life of his wife Katherine, who had died two years earlier, which will be examined in more detail below.

The authors of godly biographies and funeral sermons maintained that they did not commend the dead in order to praise them, but rather to provide examples of exceptional religious lives as patterns for imitation. Printed funeral sermons had two distinct audiences, the first being the mourners in the church and the second being the readers of a later physical text, which could both be reprinted and re-edited. In general it is almost impossible to tell how closely a preacher followed his spoken version in print. Another complexity in using funeral sermons and godly biographies as sources lies in their obviously generic nature, yet this is also one of the great values of these texts for this current enquiry. As certain religious characteristics were promoted as desirable in women from clerical households, the texts reveal the habits of female religiosity that the clergy wished to emphasise in their families and to urge their congregations to emulate. As these habits were formulated and reformulated in print they were used by the clergy to buttress the legitimacy of clerical marriage and to demonstrate to their readers the respectable reputations of their wives and daughters. After the abolition of episcopacy in 1646 printed funeral sermons were dominated by the Presbyterians and were frequently spun to demonstrate the moderation of traditional puritanism in the face of the rise of the radical sects during and after the civil wars.

According to Edmund Staunton, who preached in 1654 at the funeral of Elizabeth Wilkinson, the wife of Henry Wilkinson the principal of Magdalen Hall in Oxford under the Commonwealth, she was not accustomed to the 'affectation of high-flown phrases, but held fast the form of sound words. She was an old Disciple, and her grave and sober language accordingly discovered her so to be'. Similarly, three years later, when Henry Wilkinson preached at the funeral of Margaret Corbet, the wife of Edward Corbet, he described her as being 'one that held fast her profession without wavering. She was not carried about with every wind of doctrine'. When she met those inclined to separation she laboured to convince them of their errors and win them to the truth.[18] These remarks were made against a backdrop of enthusiastic lay participation in religious debate, encouraged both by the breakdown of censorship of the press and the activities of lay preachers both male and female, which had become increasingly apparent since the outbreak of civil war in 1642. We can take Elizabeth Avery, who was attracted to the fifth monarchists, as an example: in 1647 Avery published *Scripture Prophecies Opened*, a prophetic work in epistolatory form, in which she compared England's national church to Babylon (representing religious error) and cast herself as a prophet, who could reveal God's truth to the nation.[19] She was fiercely repudiated in print by her brother, Thomas Parker, a

New England Presbyterian minister, who complained of Elizabeth that printing a book 'above the custom of your sex, doth rankly smell'.[20]

In 1659 Edward Reynolds, who was soon to be made bishop of Norwich at the Restoration in the following year, recommended Nicholas Guy's funeral sermon for Elizabeth Gouge as one of a number of works about women that exhibited 'much provocation and encouragement to holiness', which emphasises the long-term influence of such publications.[21] Included in his list were two other publications about clergy wives, Thomas Gataker's 1638 sermon at the funeral of Joyce Featley, wife to a Royal chaplain, and the recent narrative of the life and death of Dorothy, the wife of the parliamentarian vicar of Rotherham, John Shaw.[22] When it was published in 1626 *Pieties Pillar* had marked a new departure in print by providing an extended and positive depiction of a specific clerical marriage. The preacher, Nicholas Guy, elaborated at length on themes that would become standard fare in the descriptions of other clergy wives in subsequent funeral sermons. It was published at the 'importunity' of William Gouge, who wanted to preserve the memory of his 'vertuous and religious Wife' and it should be regarded as a collaborative effort between the two men, because Elizabeth's exemplary behaviour can be mapped very closely to the idealised precepts about wives set out in William's popular conduct book *Of Domesticall Duties* first published in 1622 and reprinted three times before the civil wars. Guy tells us that Elizabeth was dutiful to her husband throughout twenty one years of marriage and she maintained both her children and servants in an obedient awe of her. She also kept St Paul's precepts to 'keepe at home' and of 'keeping silence' since she did not 'care' to go outside the home unless her husband went with her. Her prudent ordering of their household allowed William to attend to his public function and her many graces included sobriety, which graced her husband's vocation, but piety was Elizabeth's best quality.[23]

The points of contact between Guy's description of Elizabeth and her husband's conduct book are obvious. Guy explains, for example, that Elizabeth's sobriety could be seen in her behaviour and even her clothing, which reflected her sober and serious mind. In *Of Domesticall Duties*, Gouge had similarly written 'of a wife-like sobriety', which included reverencing her husband by her gesture and speech. He also wrote that a wife's modesty should be signalled by her clothing, for 'it is a token of great reverence in a wife towards her husband, to have an eye to his place and state in her apparel'. Guy tells us that Elizabeth supported her neighbours in visiting the sick and sending them food, and she set aside a part of her quarterly allowance from her husband to contribute to charitable collections. This was in accord with her husband's own advice to his readers that a husband should give an allowance to his wife so that she could make donations of her own. Just as Guy had described piety as the 'best' of Elizabeth's graces, William Gouge had urged wives to be active participants in household worship and to pray, read, teach and perform religious exercises themselves when their husbands were absent or negligent.[24] Gouge's *Of Domesticall Duties* should not therefore be interpreted as a reflection of relationships within early modern families, but like Whately's *A Bride Bush*, it was an invitation to the laity to emulate an idealised version of clerical marriage.

Guy states that Elizabeth attended to the daily exercises of religion in her household and spent time alone in the holy devotions of prayer and reading the Bible. She was also an active textual composer and wrote devout prayers and directions for devotions 'with her own hand', although Guy did not publish any of her writing. She read the Bible daily, which gave her the spiritual authority to answer readily any question about its history and doctrine. Besides bible reading she spent much of her time reading English divinity books 'whereof she had a pretty Library'.[25] The Bible has been described as the most read book in England in the early modern period, but it is only recently that the engagement of the laity with the Bible has been more fully explored. Kate Narveson has considered the impact of bible reading in the developing culture of writing from the last decades of Elizabeth's reign until the Restoration, while Femke Molekamp has investigated the ways in which female literacy agency and interpretation was grounded in responses to the Bible. Both studies draw on evidence from a wide range of writers, but neither of them considers the writing practices of women from clerical families in any depth. Narvesen asserts that 'while Reformed clergy endorsed lay scripture literacy, nowhere did they invite the laity to become writers'.[26]

This assessment seriously discounts the guidance that clerics gave to members of their own households in undertaking religious writing in a variety of forms and which they described for emulation by the laity in their publications. This was by no means a static process, but was seen by the clergy as part of a growth in religious knowledge and spiritual understanding, and it involved actively creating written texts with personal meanings. This is reflected in the advice given by the Independent divine and regicide, Hugh Peter, to his twenty year old daughter Elizabeth and published after his execution in 1660 in *A Dying Fathers Last Legacy to an Onely Child: Or Mr Hugh Peter's Advice to his Daughter*. As he neared death, Peter recommended a close and constant reading of the Bible – 'this one book' he wrote 'will answer any question'. He explained that when reading the Bible

> in every chapter, first mind the method, then note the hard things you understand not, and get helps to clear them to you. And lastly gather out the chief doctrines, or lessons, then in reading one chapter, you may understand many.

He also advised keeping a book by you

> in which, every night before you sleep, you set down on the one side, the Lords gracious providence and dealings with you; and your dealings with him on the other side: This Watch well kept, fits for Prayer, Fastings, Sabbath, Sacraments, and Death; upon which Judgment follows.[27]

Children raised in clerical households were taught to read and write, so that they could read the Bible and reflect on their own spiritual understanding and, in keeping with the conventions of the time, the early education of children was usually undertaken by their mothers. In his *Priest to the Temple* written in the 1630s and published posthumously in 1652, the poet and conformist minister, George Herbert, prioritised this work as the first duty of a cleric's wife, who should train 'her children and maids in the fear of God, with prayers and catechising and all religious duties'. Similarly, the dissenting minister, Samuel Clarke, described his wife Katherine as instilling the 'first grounds and principles of religion' into their nine children, and choosing religious maids and instructing them by 'catechising, enquiring what they remembered of the sermons they heard; reading her [sermon] notes to them'.[28] Women of other social rank including the aristocracy and the gentry also instructed their children and servants in their religious duties, but the specialised nature of an upbringing under a minister's roof was recognised in 1654 by the future Dean of Rochester, Nathaniel Hardy, when he preached the funeral sermon for Mary Smith and described her education as 'no doubt, religious' as she was the daughter of Isaac Colfe, a 'reverend minister', and her 'conversation every way corresponding to that education'. Similarly Ann Terry, the daughter of the nonconformist minister Thomas Manton, was praised after her death in 1693, because 'in all relations she answered her pious Education, as a Child, a Mother, and Wife, never any went beyond her'.[29]

The clerical household deserves to be acknowledged more widely as a focus for the education of women and as a powerhouse of female learning. The low levels of pay accorded to the post-Reformation clergy meant that some clergy wives supplemented the family income by running small-scale boarding schools for girls as well as teaching local children. As an orphan from a gentry family Elizabeth Gouge had lived for two years from *c.* 1600–2 in the house of John Huckle, the minister of Hatfield Broad Oak, Essex, whose wife 'had a great name . . .. For skill and faithful care in training up young gentlewomen'.[30] As Theodosia Alleine explained in her life of her husband the dissenting minister Joseph Alleine, she had the tuition of five or six daughters of gentlemen of 'good rank', who lodged with the Alleines in Taunton in the 1650s and were under Joseph's 'domestic oversight'. We do not know what proportion of the seventeenth-century clergy were married nor how many women were educated in their homes, but as there were approximately ten thousand parishes in England and Wales at the time it is likely that many thousands of young women were trained by the clergy during this period. Amongst their numbers were some notable advocates for female education including Rachel Speght, the first woman to intervene in the debate about the nature of women in the early seventeenth century, and two women born later in the seventeenth century – Elizabeth Elstob, the first female scholar of Old English, and Mary Astell, The Tory philosopher.[31]

Yet being the wife or daughter of a minister was no guarantee that a woman would be a shining example to others. In his will dated 1666 John Featley, a royal chaplain, complained about his 'disobedient and rebellious daughter' Anna.[32] In her manuscript diary for 4 July 1689 Mary Woodforde, the wife of Samuel Woodforde, a prebendary of Winchester Cathedral, noted 'I cannot call to mind that I was in my closet to perform my own priuate prayers' and continued by asking God to forgive 'my forgetfulness & all other my sins'.[33] Mary Woodforde is an excellent example of a clerical wife whose writing was clearly not confined to religious issues. During the years 1684–90 she used her diary to record events of national importance including the death of Charles II, Monmouth's Rebellion and the accession of William III and Mary II. Records of her husband's work as a preacher and of family events such as her son's wilful disobedience at school, her daughter's marriages and her step-son's concerns about his inheritance are interspersed with prayers and petitions for God's mercy and blessings on her family.[34]

An extreme example of a failure to meet expectations is provided in the extraordinary and painful manuscript account of his marriage by the presbyterian minister John Rastrick, who married Jane Wilson, the daughter of a prebendary of Lincoln cathedral in 1672. Rastrick believed that 'she (who was a Minister's daughter and highly descended on the Mother's Side) might make me a good and suitable wife', but he experienced great anguish when he discovered a few days after their marriage that Jane had little understanding of his spiritual conversations with her. She later took exception to her husband's attempts to address his religious reading and conversation to their two maids instead and 'family reading was much laid aside'. When Richard Baxter recommended that Jane would receive comfort by reading his *The Right Method for a Settled Peace of Conscience* (1653), Rastrick knew that his wife would not be able to comprehend the book. His despair over the 'Strangeness' of his 'spiritual Converse' with his wife, emphasises the expectations Rastrick had that as a clergyman's daughter Jane would participate in the communal reading of religious texts and discuss religious matters with him.[35]

In 1681 Richard Baxter published a life of his own wife Margaret, which was extremely unconventional in analysing the tensions in their relationship. Like Jane Rastrick, Margaret refused to lead family prayers in Baxter's absence 'Through a diseased enmitie to ostentation and hypocrisie' as Baxter glossed it. After twenty years of marriage Baxter confessed that:

> I thought the marriage of ministers had so great inconveniencies, that though necessity made it lawful, yet it was but lawful; that is to be avoided as far as lawfully we may . . . my wife lived and died in the same mind.

He also noted that he did not marry until 1662, when he was 'silenced and ejected, and had no flock or pastoral cure'. This work was reprinted in 1683 by Baxter's friend Samuel Clarke in his final omnibus edition of godly lives, *The Lives of Sundry Eminent Persons in this Later Age*, together with Samuel's life of his own wife Katherine. Samuel chose to excise these and some other contentious comments about Margaret from Baxter's book when he published it.[36]

Clarke preferred, like many of his fellow clergymen, to offer the seventeenth-century reading public an idealised image of the clerical family in which the conduct of their wives and daughters was worthy of emulation. They emphasised the encouragement they gave to these women to read improving books of practical piety in English and to avoid the influence of unedifying works. The wills of the seventeenth-century parish clergy reinforced this educational bias and, if books are mentioned, English works of practical piety were left to wives and daughters while it was sons who were usually given works in Latin and other foreign languages.[37] Individual clergy daughters were depicted in print as shunning frivolous reading material. Thus Ann Terry, who married into a merchant family, advised her own children to

> spend time every day in reading God's word . . . do not squander your time in reading plays and romances, and filthy books, which will corrupt your fancies, and make you unfit for the service of God.[38]

Similarly, Elizabeth Dunton, the daughter of the dissenting minister Samuel Annesley and sister to the more famous Susannah Wesley, furnished her closet with the Bible and practical books instead of 'dead, lifeless formularies, play-books and romances' as her husband, John, noted after her death in 1697. John Dunton was a London publisher of devotional works, sermons and periodicals, who was descended from three successive generations of clerics on the paternal side of his family, and he wrote his tribute to his wife in the familiar format of the godly biography, many of which he himself had printed.[39]

Some women from clerical families did receive a more extensive education, but when this was described in print the emphasis by the clergy was on the predominance of their religious training. After her parents separated at the start of the seventeenth century, Elizabeth Joceline was raised in the home of her maternal grandfather William Chaderton, the Bishop of Lincoln, where she was taught languages, including Latin, history and 'some arts', but principally studies of piety.[40] Elizabeth Bury, who was born in the mid-1640s, was described by her husband, Samuel, the presbyterian minister at Bury St Edmunds, as learning Hebrew so well that she could quote from original texts and she learned French in order to talk to French Protestant refugees. She also studied a range of subjects including philosophy, history, mathematics, anatomy and medicine. Yet her husband insisted that her 'constant, favourite and darling study was divinity, especially the Holy Scriptures'.[41]

Funeral sermons and godly lives depict clergy wives and daughters as active readers and writers, and the authors of these works explicitly invited other women to emulate them in developing their religious writing practices. When Katherine Clarke died Samuel Clarke recovered not only sermon notes, but also transcripts of biblical passages and a religious commonplace book in her cabinet. By the time that Katherine was writing, the commonplace method of making notes from other sources under various headings had long been recommended in the works of educational theorists and religious writers. As Kevin Sharpe observes, although these authors set out suggested headings for their readers to use, this method of collating written information made every educated Englishman or woman 'into a reader who very much made his or her own meaning'.[42] Thus Anne Terry connected her reading to her own personal religious experiences and she marked passages in her own Bible and books that particularly concerned herself 'under the variety of the dispensations that she passed through'. Anne was a conscientious reader of the Bible and wrote out passages of the Scriptures with 'profitable remarks' on them for her own religious use.[43]

Katherine Clarke described her own reading and writing habits as part of her highly personalised search for a comfortable assurance 'of my eternal and everlasting salvation'. Katherine described how childhood vanities had 'cooled' her faith, but her father, Valentine Overton, Rector of Bedworth in Warwickshire, had instructed her to write sermon notes and to learn the catechism of William Perkins, the eminent Elizabethan puritan theologian. This practice preserved and strengthened her faith and, according to Samuel Clarke, Katherine continued to write sermon notes throughout her life 'to prevent drowsiness and distractions and to help memory, whereof she hath left many volumes'. She also made use of these sermon notes by frequently reading and meditating on them, and she read a portion of the Scriptures and of the psalms daily 'and took special notice of such passages as most concerned herself'. As part of this integrated programme of reading and writing, she transcribed biblical texts, which she read in times of temptation or desertion. Just as Hugh Peter had recommended, she also kept 'a little book', in which she gave an account of 'God's gracious dealings with her', including sickness, the deaths of 'my dear children', times of 'spiritual desertion' and when 'I have been under great fears in the time of our civil wars'.[44]

There are strong parallels between Samuel Clarke's depiction of Katherine's writing and Anthony Walker's portrayal of his wife's reading and writing practices, although the individual approaches of the two women are also apparent. Walker was a conformist Essex minister, who published a funeral sermon in 1678 for his patroness Mary Rich, the Countess of Warwick, which included extracts from her spiritual diary and meditations entitled *The Virtuous Woman Found, Her Loss bewayl'd, and Character Exemplified*.[45] When his own wife Elizabeth died he published material from her papers, which he considered useful for 'the promoting God's interest in the world' in *The Vertuous Wife or, the Holy Life of Mrs Elizabeth Walker* (1690). The similarities between the two titles indicate the spiritual equality that Walker accorded to the two women in spite of the social gulf between them and he quoted from Elizabeth's meditations, letters and large octavo book 'of the best Paper she could buy, neatly bound, gilded, and ruled with red', in which she had written some memorials of 'God's providences' to herself and her family. Neither Katherine Clarke nor Elizabeth Walker was depicted by her husband as a serene, untroubled Christian and, just as Katherine wrote of her feelings of temptation and desertion, Elizabeth records that before her marriage 'I had temptations that there was no God, which was very vexatious to me'. She spent six months with the family of John Beadle, the minister of Branston in Essex, where she spent time in reading and secret prayer, and 'ate sparingly'. Anthony Walker describes this as a period when his wife was assailed by Satan with horrid suggestions and blasphemous temptations. Later as a married woman, Elizabeth developed a daily round of religious reading and observance. She read the Scriptures privately in the morning and spent an hour or more in the afternoon reading good books. She prepared for taking communion by privately reading 'the best books of that subject' or by reading them in the family to prepare their servants for the sacrament. Elizabeth also drew on her 'Memorials' as well as her instructions and religious directions for their two surviving daughters. Anthony quoted from her papers, which he found in the drawer of her writing table and he framed this as evidence of her modesty, because she would slide her book or papers into the drawer when he entered her closet. On one occasion she had extracted a promise from him never to look at them while she was alive.[46]

Similarly, Samuel Bury reproduced some of the writing of his wife Elizabeth, who was the step-daughter of Nathaniel Bradshaw, the rector of Willingham in Cambridgeshire. Samuel maintained that he quoted from her writing verbatim, but did not have space to publish all of her work, which he published not, as he said, to glorify her name, but in order to preserve her memory and to 'propagate' religion in the world. Elizabeth used her diaries to review her spiritual state and recorded that she had first begun 'the work of self-examination' under Bradshaw's roof when she was nine or ten years old in the early 1650s and dated her religious conversion to that time. She began to keep 'an account of the trials of myself' in a diary 1670 when she was aged 25 and in 1690 she used this to review her spiritual state during the past twenty years. Samuel Bury emphasised the importance she placed on this process for 'the review of former experiences was an extraordinary help to future confidence . . .and hence it was she often recommended this practice to others'. Like Elizabeth Walker, Elizabeth Bury was concerned about other people reading her private writing and she used an indecipherable shorthand in her diaries for twenty years. In 1690 she began to use longhand in the diaries, which allowed Samuel to publish extracts from them and from some of her letters when she died in 1720.[47]

There is clearly a balance in these descriptions by the clergy between the authority that their female relatives derived from their knowledge of the Bible and the need to maintain the respectability of the clerical household. Elizabeth Joceline's posthumously published work the *Mother's Legacie to her Unborn Child* (1624) was a conventional book that addressed the education of her unborn child. Like much of the writing of other women from clergy families, the manuscript of the *Legacie* was found in Elizabeth's desk after her death (in childbirth). It was prepared for the press by Thomas Goad, a Cambridge theologian and chaplain to the Archbishop of Canterbury, who licenced its publication. Goad had known Elizabeth as a child in the bishop's home and commended her for wearing her learning lightly, because she was 'sparing in her discourses' about her knowledge, 'possessing it rather to hide, than to boast of'.[48]

In similar vein, Edmund Staunton described Elizabeth Wilkinson as having 'the ornament of a meek and quiet spirit' and offered her as 'a rare Example of many thousands, a choyce patterne for imitation'. She was careful to remember what she heard and 'took much pains in writing Sermons, and collecting speciall Notes out of practical Divines'. Yet Elizabeth could both assert God's truth and convince 'gainsayers'. Her usual custom was 'to move good discourse, and oft times turne the streame of other impertinent discourses into somewhat, which was solid, tending to edification, and administering grace unto the hearer'. Staunton published a paper in Elizabeth's own hand describing her religious convictions and growth as a Christian, in which she described her feelings of temptation to sin as a teenager. She had thoughts of atheism, 'which were most terrible unto me' and left her with 'such a terrour upon my spirit, as made me fear that I had committed that *sin against the Holy Ghost*'. Her reading of Calvin's *Institutes* and works by Henry Scudder helped to remove these fears.[49]

Henry Wilkinson's 1657 funeral sermon for Margaret Corbet may well have been influenced by Staunton's eulogy for Elizabeth as he uses very similar phraseology to describe Margaret as having attained a

> measure of Divine knowledge, as enabled her to state some Questions of controversy for her better use, and help of her memory, and to discourse very soundly upon the most material points of Religion, and even above her age and sexe, to maintain the truth . . . with strength of Argument against gain-sayers.[50]

Some husbands gave examples of their wives using their apparent modesty to rebuke others and even to guide the clergy. Thus Elizabeth Walker sent a book to a young minister, who had been one of her husband's scholars and had lived with them for several years. Anthony tells us that the young man had shown prejudice and was at first averse to Elizabeth's 'strict example' and 'serious counsels', but after a year had come to value her advice and to defer to her. In her accompanying letter she asked him to excuse the freedom with which she had written to him and acknowledged that he was 'much more knowing and conversant with books, especially that which excells all others, the Holy Scriptures'.[51] Samuel Bury described his wife, Elizabeth, smartly correcting younger people and her inferiors with severity, but others she rebuked with 'much gentleness, meekness and modesty'. She also reproved clerics with a certain 'freedom' as her husband phrased it, but ameliorated her remarks by prefacing them with the biblical verse 1 Timothy 5:1 'rebuke not an elder, but entreat him as a father, and the younger men as brethren'.[52]

These vignettes should not be interpreted as evidence of female transgressive behaviour, but instead they were illustrative of the spiritual authority that these women had acquired through their religious knowledge and status as clergy wives. George Herbert had advocated for the parson's wife to be 'the beginner of all good discourses' among her neighbours. His children and servants were to play a similar role amongst their counterparts 'so that as in the house of those that are skilled in music, all are musicians, so in the house of a preacher, all are preachers'. By this he did not mean to encourage women to enter the pulpit to preach, but rather to make their life an example and act of edification to others. Nearly a century after the publication of Herbert's *Priest to the Temple* in 1652, John Wesley, the leading Methodist, described his mother Susanna in very similar terms. Reflecting on her death in 1742 he wrote 'I cannot but farther observe that even she – as well as her father and grandfather, her husband and her three sons – had been, in her measure and degree, a preacher of righteousness'.[53] These statements demonstrate an acceptance of female spiritual authority within the bounds of the clerical household.

We cannot fully understand the clerical estate in the early modern period unless we also consider how the clergy represented the integration of their wives and daughters into their households in their publications. In order to consolidate the status of clerical marriage, the clergy had an insistent message in their conduct books, treatises on marriage, funeral sermons, godly lives and other works that marriage was a lawful and honourable estate for all men and women. Godly biographies of women from clerical families served to reinforce the legitimacy and benefits of clergy marriage and their subjects were described as paragons of female virtue, ripe for emulation. So Nicholas Guy tells his readers that throughout twenty one years of marriage, Elizabeth Gouge, acted as a 'pious, prudent, provident, painfull, carefull, faithfull, helpful, grave, modest, sober, tender, loving Wife, Mother, Mistris, [and] Neighbour'. Thomas Gataker described Joyce, the wife of a royal chaplain to Charles I Daniel Featley, as 'one of a thousand; a compleat Woman, a compleat wife; Defective in nothing, that might be required in either'.[54] Dorothy Shaw was commended for her 'humility, mildnesse, modesty, and discretion, excelling therein most of her sex that I ever knew, or heard of' by Nicholas Heathcote, pastor of Rowley in Yorkshire, in one of a series of five letters of commendation from fellow ministers to her husband and published in his biography of her. As counterparts to his wife, John Shaw noted how 'our *Chronicles* commend the wife of Archbishop *Parker* as a great example of humility, chastity, fidelity' and cited Magdalen the wife of the German theologian Dr. David Pareus, 'for that, after she was maried, and 40. years of age, out of love to the Scriptures, she learned to read, and took such delight in the word, that she got much of it by heart'.[55]

At the heart of this perfection lay the exceptional religious and educational guidance provided by the clergy to their wives, daughters and other women in their households, which they also promoted to other social groups through their publications. The clergy not only intermarried, but they also chose their spouses from the ranks of the gentry and merchant classes, creating wider circles of godly influence and education and consolidating the status of clergy families as intimately connected to these other social groups. These links were often stressed in the sources considered here, which further reinforced the respectability of the clergy family. Henry Wilkinson wrote of Margaret Corbet, the daughter of the ecclesiastical lawyer Sir Nathaniel Brent and granddaughter of bishop Robert Abbott of Salisbury, that 'If we enquire into the Relations of our deceased sister, either by *Affinity* or *Consanguinity* on both sides, the families are ancient, of renowne and good reputation'. Elizabeth Walker described her father John Sadler as 'an Eminent Citizen' and London grocer, who traded in drugs and tobacco while her mother Elizabeth, was the daughter of Mr Dackum minister of Portsmouth. Clergy wives were also depicted as performing the traditional obligations of the gentry including making charitable donations on their own behalf and acting as a physician to their neighbours. Anthony Walker described his wife preparing medicines for the family, the poor and the neighbourhood – 'she distilled waters, syrups, oils, ointment, salves etc to distribute them out'.[56] Joyce Featley acted as both physician and apothecary to the poor and gave them waters, medicines and advice.[57] The clergy family was not a closed unit, but shared close ties of kinship and social obligations with their merchant and gentry relations.

During the seventeenth century these ties became ever denser in a second phase for the institution of clerical marriage. At the same time clerical dynasties became more numerous and they furnished candidates for high office and parish livings alike. These developments helped to consolidate the clergy family as a respectable social institution and as a powerhouse of female literacy, and at the same time the clergy also invited the laity to imitate the clerical family through the reading of their conduct books and marriage sermons. From the 1620s the clergy further extended the growing popularity of funeral sermons and godly lives to include their own wives and daughters as examples of exceptionally virtuous and religiously educated women, who were worthy of imitation. These publications certainly created an idealised image of clerical marriage that did not always match the experience of the clergy, as we have seen. Nevertheless, it was an image which served to move the focus of the printed word from debate about clerical marriage to its emulation during the century from 1620 to 1720.

## Notes

1 H. Parish, *Clerical Marriage and the English Reformation: Precedent, Policy and Practice* (Aldershot, 2000); E. J. Carlson, 'Clerical Marriage and the English Reformation', in *Journal of British Studies*, vol 31 (1992), pp. 1–31; P. Sherlock, 'Monuments, Reputation and Clerical Marriage in Reformation England: Bishop Barlow's Daughters', in *Gender and History*, vol 16 (2004), pp. 57–82; see also R. Basch, 'The Changing Status and Identity of English Bishops' Wives, *c.* 1549–1625', University of London PhD thesis, 2016.

2 A. Thompson, *Parish Clergy Wives in Elizabethan England* (Leiden, 2019).

3 The only extensive manuscript collection is that of Sarah Savage, who was born in 1664 and was the eldest daughter of the dissenting minister Philip Henry, see Cheshire Archives and Local Studies, Basten Manuscripts, diary of Sarah Savage 1686–1688, Z/D/Basten/8; Bodleian Library, Miscellaneous English Mss., copy of Sarah Savage's diary from 1714–1723, Misc. e. 331; Dr Williams's Library, Henry Manuscripts, copy of Sarah Savage's diary for 1743–8, Henry Mss. 90.2. See also J. B. Williams (ed.), *Memoirs of the Life and Character of Mrs Sarah Savage . . . To which are added, Memoirs of the Life and Character of Mrs Anne Hulton and Mrs Eleanor Radford* (Philadelphia, undated).

4 Cited in P. Collinson, *The Religion of Protestants: the Church in English Society 1559 to 1625* (Oxford, 1982), p. 92; H. Wilkinson, *The Hope of Glory, Or, Christs Indwelling in True Believers is an Evident Demonstration of their Hope of Glory* (Oxford, 1657) p. 79.

5 Peter Du Moulin, *A Sermon Preach'd in St Martins Church . . . at the Funeral of the Right Honourable Mabella Lady Fordwitch* (London, 1669), pp. 5, 9.

6 M. Prior, 'Reviled and Crucified Marriages: The Position of Tudor Bishops' Wives' in M. Prior (ed.), *Women in English Society, 1500–1800* (London, 1985), pp. 118–48; Canterbury Cathedral Archives and Library, High Commission Papers, Deposition of Marie Taylor against Katharine Horton, 9 April 1588; F. G. Emmison, *Elizabethan Life: Morals and the Church Courts* (Chelmsford, 1973), p. 215.

7 W. Whately, *A Care-Cloth: Or A Treatise of the Cumbers and Troubles of Marriage* (1624), pp. 22–3.

8 T. Taylor, *A Good Husband and a Good Wife* (London, 1625), p. 7.

9 W. Durham, *The Life and Death of that Judicious Divine, and Accomplish'd Preacher, Robert Harris, D.D. Late President of Trinity Colledge in Oxon* (London, 1660), p. 77.

10 T. Hodges, *A Treatise of Marriage* (London, 1673), pp. 12–13.

11 G. Stanhope, *A Sermon Preach'd in St. Paul's Cathedral* (London, 1697), p. 10.

12 S. Ashe, *Gray Hayres Crowned with Grace. A Sermon Preached at Redriff, Aug. 1. 1654. at the Funerall of that Reverend, Eminently Learned and Faithfull Minister of Jesus Christ Mr Thomas Gataker* (London, 1654), pp. 49–50.

13 J. Howes, *Real Comforts, Extracted from Moral and Spiritual Principles. Presented in a Sermon, Preached at the Funeral of that Reverend Divine Mr. Thomas Ball* (London, 1659), pp. 48–9.

14 Hodges, *A Treatise of Marriage*, pp. 68–9.

15 W. Whately, *A Bride-Bush: Or a Direction for Married Persons* (London, 1619), leafs A1r–A2v. Quotations are taken from the second edition rather than the previous edition of 1617 which Whately repudiated in 1619.

16 P. Marshall, *Beliefs and the Dead in Reformation England* (Oxford, 2002); J. Eales, 'Funeral Sermons over Time: From Catholic to Protestant in the British Isles' in P. Booth and E. Tingle (eds), *Brill Companion to Death, Burial and Remembrance in Late Medieval and Early Modern Europe 1300–1700* (Leiden, forthcoming); see also P. Delany, *British Autobiography in the Seventeenth Century* (London, 1969), A. Stewart, *The Oxford History of Life-Writing: Early Modern* (Oxford, 2018); K. Sharpe and S. N. Zwicker (eds), *Writing Lives: Biography and Textuality, Identity and Representation in Early Modern England* (Oxford, 2008).

17 R. Houlbrooke, *Death, Religion and the Family in England 1480–1750* (Oxford, 1998), pp. 306–10; see also F. B. Tromly, '"According to Sounde Religion": The Elizabethan Controversy over the Funeral Sermon', in *Journal of Medieval and Renaissance Studies* vol 13, no 2 (1983) pp. 293–312; E. J. Carlson, 'English Funeral Sermons as Sources: The Example of Female Piety in Pre-1640 Sermons,' in *Albion* vol 32, no 4 (2000), 567–97; F. Molekamp, 'Seventeenth-Century Funeral Sermons and Exemplary Female Devotion: Gendered Spaces and Histories', in *Renaissance and Reformation* vol 35, no 1 (2012) pp. 43–63.

18 E. Staunton *A Sermon Preacht at Great Milton in the County of Oxford . . . at the Funeral of that Eminent Servant of Jesus Christ Mris. Elizabeth Wilkinson* (Oxford, 1659) p. 35; Wilkinson, *The Hope of Glory*, pp. 67–9.

19 E. Avery, *Scripture Prophecies Opened* (London, 1647), pp. 1, 2, 4, see also Jane Baston, 'Elizabeth Avery (fl. 1614–53)' in *ODNB*.

20 T. Parker, *The Visions and Prophecies of Daniel Expounded* (London, 1646), idem, *The Copy of a Letter Written by Mr Thomas Parker* (London, 1650), leaf A2, p. 13.

21 E. Reynolds, *Imitation and Caution for Christian Woman: or, The Life and Death of that Excellent Gentlewoman, Mrs. Mary Bewley* (London: 1659), p. 2.

22 T. Gataker, *Saint Stevens Last Will and Testament* (London, 1638); J. Shaw, *Mistris Shawe's Tomb-stone or, the Saints Remains* (London, 1658).

23 N. Guy, *Pieties Pillar: Or a Sermon Preached at the Funerall of Mistresse Elizabeth Gouge* (London, 1626), leaf A3r–v.

24 William Gouge, *Of Domesticall Duties, Eight Treatises* (London, 1622), pp. 277–80, 403–4, 260.

25 Guy, *Pieties Pillar: Or a Sermon Preached at the Funerall of Mistresse Elizabeth Gouge*, pp. 39–49.

26 K. Narveson, *Bible Readers and Lay Writers in Early Modern England: Gender and Self-definition in an Emergent Writing Culture* (Farnham, 2012) p. 9; F. Molekamp, *Women and the Bible in Early Modern England: Religious Reading and Writing* (Oxford, 2013).

27 Hugh Peter, *A Dying Fathers Last Legacy to an Onely Child: Or Mr Hugh Peter's Advice to his Daughter* (London, 1660), pp. 1–14.

28 G. Herbert, *A Priest to the Temple; or the Country Parson* (London, 1652), pp. 38–42; S. Clarke, *A Looking-Glass for Good Women to Dress Themselves by: held Forth in the Life and Death of Mrs Katherine Clarke* (London, 1677), pp. 21–3.

29 N. Hardy, *Death's Alarum Or, Security's Warning Piece* (London, 1654), p. 31; T. Manton, *Advice to Mourners Under the Loss of Relations* (London, 1693), p. viii.

30 Guy, *Pieties Pillar: Or a Sermon Preached at the Funerall of Mistresse Elizabeth Gouge*, pp. 39–49.

31 B. Lewalski, *The Polemics and Poems of Rachel Speght* (Oxford, 1996); M. Gretsch, 'Elizabeth Elstob (1683–1756)' in *ODNB*; for Astell's training by her clerical uncle see S. Apetrei, *Women, Feminism and Religion in Early Enlightenment England* (Cambridge, 2010), pp. 79–85.

32 See Stephen Wright, 'John Featley (1604/5–1667) in *ODNB*.

33 New College Archives, Oxford (hereinafter NCA), Woodforde Papers, Mary Woodforde's Book, (1684–1690) 9507 f. 38r. I am grateful to Sophie Butler for providing me with a transcript of the diary from which these extracts are taken.

34 NCA 9507, ff. 1r, 4v, 12r, 35v,41r.

35 A. Cambers (ed.), *The Life of John Rastrick, 1650–1727*, Camden 5th Series, vol 36 (Cambridge, 2010), pp. 83, 184–9.

36 R. Baxter, *A Breviate of the Life of Margaret . . . Wife of Richard Baxter* (London, 1681), pp. 79, 101–2; Clarke's reprint is to be found in S. Clarke, *The Lives of Sundry Eminent Persons in this Later Age* (London, 1683), pp. 181–91.

37 J. Eales, 'Female Literacy and the Social Identity of the Clergy Family in the Seventeenth Century', in *Archaeologia Cantiana*, vol 133, (2013) p. 70.

38 T. Alleine, *The Life and Death of Mr. Joseph Alleine* (London, 1672) leaf A4r; Manton, *Advice to Mourners*, p. 49.

39 J. Dunton, *An Essay Proving We Shall Know our Friends in Heaven* (London, 1698), pp. 25–6.

40 E. Joceline, *The Mother's Legacie, to her unborne Childe* (London, 1624), leaf ar-v.

41 S. Bury, *An Account of the Life and Death of Mrs Elizabeth Bury* (London, 1720), p. 6.

42 K. Sharpe, *The Politics of Reading in Early Modern* England (New Haven, 2000) p. 41; see also Cambers, *Godly Reading*, pp. 30–33.

43 Manton, *Advice to Mourners*, p. xiv.

44 Clarke, *A Looking-Glass for Good Women*, pp. 7–11, 15, 16, 39, 43, 44–5, 48–9, 85. Katherine's eulogy appears in Samuel Clarke, *The Lives of Sundry Eminent Persons in the Later Age* (1683) part II, pp. 165–159 (p. 159 misnumbered).

45 A. Walker, *The Virtuous Woman Found, Her Loss bewayl'd, and Character Exemplified in a Sermon Preach't at Felsted in Essex, at the Funeral of the Most Excellent and Religious Lady, the Right Honourable Mary Countess Dowager of Warwick* (London, 1678). See also R. Anselment, *The Occasional Meditations of Mary Rich, Countess of Warwick* (Tempe, 2009).

46 A. Walker, *The Vertuous Wife or, the Holy Life of Mrs Elizabeth* Walker (London, 1690) pp. 5, 6, 17–23, 72, 83.

47 Bury, *An Account of the Life and Death of Mrs Elizabeth Bury*, pp. 53, 11.

48 Joceline, *The Mother's Legacie, to her Unborne Childe*, leaf A1r–v.

49 Staunton *A Sermon Preacht at Great Milton in the County of Oxford*, pp. 23–36.

50 Wilkinson, *The Hope of Glory*, pp. 64–5.

51 Walker, *The Vertuous Wife*, pp. 248–57.

52 Bury, *Life and Death of Mrs Elizabeth Bury*, p. 50.

53 C. Wallace (ed.), *Susanna Wesley, The Complete Writings* (Oxford, 1997), p. 14.

54 Gataker, *Saint Stevens Last Will and Testament*, p. 26.

55 Shaw, *Mistris Shawe's Tomb-stone or, the Saints Remains* p. leaf b1r, pp. 72–3.

56 Wilkinson, *The Hope of Glory*, p. 62; Walker, *The Vertuous Wife*, pp. 9–12, 35.

57 Gataker, *Saint Stevens Last Will and Testament*, p. 27.

# FINANCES OF THE ANGLICAN EPISCOPATE IN THE EIGHTEENTH CENTURY

William Gibson, Oxford Brookes University

The scholarship on episcopal finances in the eighteenth century is thin. It is largely confined to the studies of institutional finance or to biographical studies of individual bishops. Of the former, both G. F. A. Best and Norman Sykes have shown that episcopal finances were unequal and that this caused problems in specific cases.[1] The individual studies of bishops, inevitably, do not assess whether a bishop's wealth or poverty was representative, and rarely consider whether it was due to skill – or its absence – in financial management. This paper aims to give a more systematic examination of the problems of episcopal income and expenditure in the eighteenth century and to suggest that while these were significant, they were, in many cases, not simply neglected by bishops.

Bishops, as the most senior and usually the most affluent of the clergy, are assumed to have lived lives of financial ease, and the assumption is often that – in acquiring a mitre – bishops found economic security. There are certainly examples of extremely wealthy bishops in the period. Bishops Thomas Sherlock of London was said to have left £100,000 in his will and his predecessor, Edmund Gibson, left a similarly large sum.[2] Bishop Shute Barrington left £160,000.[3] Bishop Sherlock's estate was so large that it shocked many and he was satirised in a print entitled 'Blessed be the Lord for I am Rich.'[4]

But rich bishops were the exceptions, remarkable because of the amount they left. More common was the experience of Bishop Benjamin Hoadly. Hoadly came from a poor family but had been a bishop from 1716 for forty years, the last twenty as incumbent of the wealthy see of Winchester. He left the relatively small sum of £17,000, having spent huge sums on charities and donations.[5] Bishop Richard Trevor already had a substantial private income, though he left a very modest sum of £3,450, having spent much on buildings during his episcopate.[6] Some bishops were rash with their money, such as Bishop Joseph Butler of Durham who was shocked to find that he had £500 in his house and ordered it all to be given to the

https://doi.org/10.16922/jrhlc.6.2.3

"Blessed be the Lord for I am Rich" anonymous mezzotint *c.* 1734, depicting Bishop Thomas Sherlock. From the collection of William Gibson and reproduced with permission.

poor.[7] On occasion bishops left their families destitute, in part because they did not wish to use their episcopal incomes for private purposes. Bishop Gilbert Burnet of Salisbury said that he would be 'guilty of the greatest crime if he raised fortunes for his children out of the revenues of his bishopric.'[8] However there was a contemporary expectation of provision for descendants, and not to do so presented problems. For example, Bishop John Conybeare of Bristol died so poor in 1755 that his fellow bishops were obliged to petition the King, George II, for a pension for his widow.[9] And Bishop Charles Trimnell of Winchester died leaving his family almost destitute and forced to rely on his son for an income. After his death, Hoadly's widow was forced to print copies of her husband's portrait to raise money to live on.[10] A part of the problems for the eighteenth-century Church was the complex system of income and expenditure for bishops.

## Income

One problem with episcopal incomes was their unevenness. There were some very wealthy bishoprics, including the two archbishoprics and sees of Durham, Winchester, and London, which each had an income of above £10,000 per annum. At the opposite end of the spectrum were the poorest dioceses, notably Oxford, Bristol and those in Wales, which brought in less than £500 per annum – not much more than a good parish living. This reflected their historic land ownership and endowments. Moreover incomes fluctuated with land values, and such variables as the exploitation of mineral rights, the drainage of marshland and the cycle of lease renewal fines. And bishops were not chosen for their abilities as effective managers of their estates; the income from a diocese could collapse if it was not well maintained.[11] In addition, some bishops faced a battle to repair the financial neglect of a predecessor.

The government recognised the seriousness of the problem and usually permitted bishops who were appointed to the poorer dioceses to retain other posts to increase their incomes.[12] These were called livings held *in commendam*. For example, it was almost a convention that the bishop of Rochester, with an income of just £600 a year, routinely also held the deanery of Westminster, which increased the income. The bishops of Oxford and Bristol were almost always permitted to hold canonries in St Paul's or elsewhere to support their incomes. This also meant that they could live in the houses attached to the canonries when they resided in London.

But *commendams* were always the subject of tension: on the one hand bishops could not appear too greedy, and also the government also wanted to share out clerical appointments and maximise the benefits of patronage. But in the eighteenth century, the issue of *commendams* sometimes threatened an episcopal appointment. In 1772 John Moore, the dean of Canterbury, stated candidly to Lord Eden that the prime minister, Lord North, 'must understand I will not be a Bishop unless he contrives I may live with some degree of comfort, I mean without such an income as may enable me to support my station.'[13] Equally, in 1719 John Potter refused preferment because it was said he was 'easy in his present preferments'.[14]

The four Welsh dioceses, each with extremely low incomes were particularly unattractive. Dean Green of Lincoln in 1761 declined the bishopric of St David's on the grounds that it was worth no more than a few hundred pounds a year and without 'tolerable *commendam*' would not attract a clergyman.[15] It was only with the greatest reluctance that Joseph Butler, who had been raised as the son of a draper, accepted the see of Bristol, which yielded just four hundred pounds a year, and had to be augmented with the rectory of Stanhope *in commendam*.[16] Not all clergy could dictate terms in this way: the wealthy Dean Graham of Carlisle declined the offer of Carlisle diocese in 1702 because he insisted that he should retain his prebend of Durham in *commendam* and the government refused to allow it.[17] Occasionally a bishop might be offered a way to increase his income. Martin Benson, bishop of Gloucester (1735–1752) was offered a parish living by Lord Huntingdon in 1737, to augment his low income. He was obliged to reply to Huntingdon thanking him for the offer but indicating that he could not accept an additional living from Huntingdon as bishops were restricted from doing so by the terms of their *commendams* from the crown.[18]

Once appointed to a diocese, a bishop had to manage his estates so as to ensure he had an adequate income. An example of how complex the management of episcopal estates could be is revealed in Bishop Hoadly's survey of the finances of Salisbury diocese which he conducted between 1723 and 1734. One issue was the range of sources of income for the bishopric. In many cases the payment of income from the episcopal estates came in the form of agricultural produce, just as clergy received tithes. Hoadly received some payments in the form of bushels of wheat, loads of straw, and in some cases the sale of wood from forests. There were rental and lease incomes from farms, and also from urban tenements that were owned by the bishopric, as well as some small customary payments, often listed as 'pensions'. Some of these were tiny amounts of money, many as small as a shilling, that were probably individually not worth the cost of collection, but which together made up over fifty pounds per annum towards the bishopric. One of the issues related to the collection of income was the complex nature of the payment schedules: some items were paid annually, some quarterly, others biannually – the latter using the traditional payment cycles of Lady Day and Michaelmas. Moreover the episcopal estates spread beyond the boundaries of the diocese of Salisbury, so that there were properties in Berkshire and Dorset that were not in the diocese of Salisbury and in Berkshire the bishop had to rely on the archdeacon of another diocese to collect the income. The bishops of Salisbury were also, by tradition, chancellors of the Order of the Garter, which yielded an additional salary of £100 a year together with some allowances for paper and a house at Windsor. But there were of course costs in attendance at Garter events and in discharging the role of chancellor at court which were rarely covered by the income.

Hoadly's accounts made clear that some forms of income were 'uncertain sums' which fluctuated, sometimes so wildly that they could only be accounted on a ten-year cycle. Foremost among these was the income from fines – the payments made on the renewal of a lease. These depended on the chance and circumstances of a lease renewal or, if the lease was agreed on the terms of three lives, the longevity of the leaseholder. Bishop John Hough of Worcester, when he was very old, said that his tenants expected that he would 'snap at what they offer' since they calculated that he would not have long to live and therefore would not want a long and protracted lease-renewal negotiation.[19]

Woodland and forestry income was dependent on very long cycles, not just the growth of trees but also the state of the market for timber, both for naval building and house construction. Fee income from the Garter chancellorship arose from the duties on the death of a knight and was therefore also occasional rather than predictable. Over ten years, Hoadly recorded an income from Garter duties of over a thousand pounds, but none of this could have been predicted and budgeted for.[20]

There were a number of perquisites of the office of bishop, some of which were a matter of custom and practice in different dioceses. In some dioceses, until the formation of Queen Anne's Bounty, first fruits were paid by parish clergy to the bishop. In the diocese of Bangor and elsewhere, mortuary fees were paid to the bishop. There were some legal fees for consistory court cases which were paid to the bishop. But all these were forms of income that could not be predicted or relied upon. Consequently, it would not be possible for a bishop to plan his income with precision.

A second example of the financial problems facing an eighteenth-century bishop can be seen in the case of Charles Moss, bishop of St David's from 1766 to 1773. The diocese of St David's was one of the poorest and with the slowest growth in income over the century. It also suffered from extreme fluctuations of income, from £600 to below £400. Low finances had dogged the see, resulting in the exhaustion of bishops' incomes from time to time. Bishop George Bull (1705–10) had continued to pay for food to paupers in the diocese despite the extremely perilous state of his finances.[21] Bishop Adam Ottley found that his finances were so serious that he appointed his son as diocesan registrar to enable him to survive. Ottley had spent a lot of money repairing the palace at Abergwili.[22] On his death, Ottley's tenants owed him 110% of his average annual income.[23] He died in considerable debt.[24] Consequently when

Charles Moss was appointed to St David's, one of his first actions was to draw up a schedule of the finances of the see.[25] The income of the bishops was principally from two sources: the alienated tithes of twenty-three parishes in the diocese and the episcopal estates – the latter in eighty-nine separate pieces of land. Some of Bishop Moss's policies undoubtedly worked to his disadvantage; he tended to avoid ejection of tenants where possible and also renewed leases in the case of widows who wanted to continue their husbands' tenancies.[26] Where tenants found themselves in financial difficulty, Moss accepted payment in kind rather than insisting on cash payments.

Moss resisted temptation and pressure to abuse lease renewals which had the effect of robbing a successor. This could be done in two ways: first to bring forward a renewal before the expiry of the lease, which meant that the renewal fine was also brought forward from the future; and secondly to raise the fine but drop the annual rent payment. This too was a way of achieving immediate income at the expense of the longer term. Moss's insistence on a fair system meant that leasees complained, especially when they could no longer use this system for their own advantage. In a number of cases, Moss offered longer leases to tenants to ensure that future rent payments (from which he would not necessarily benefit) were stabilised.[27] Moss also standardised payment days to either biannual or annual payments.

A further serious problem facing the diocese of St David's was confusion over the extent of land ownership and demarcation. This was especially open to abuse by tenants when they had enjoyed long tenancies. In one case, the elderly landowner Damaris Roberts had so confused the extent of her own land and the bishop's leased property that a survey had to be undertaken to clarify the issue. Such surveys were undertaken on a number of occasions.[28] The complexity of acreage calculation (in Wales there were three systems of acreage measurement, one dating back to pre-Norman times) meant that Moss was obliged to employ a 'land umpire' specifically for the purpose.[29] This enabled perambulations to take place which in one case revealed that the property had been eroded over time by about ten acres. Moss's reforms of the diocesan finances of St David's were to bear fruit in the longer term with a steadily rising income for the bishops. His actions staunched the haemorrhage of the income of the diocese. Such actions were desperately in need in other dioceses. For example the income of Chester diocese fell from £1,250 in 1722 to less than half that sum in 1762.[30]

## Expenditure

On the other side of the balance sheet was a host of expenses which were not tractable. Foremost among a bishop's expenses was the cost of becoming a bishop – it was a costly business. For those clergy without financial independence the nomination to a diocese brought a crippling financial burden. From the moment of his nomination, a bishop-elect was piled high with fees and charges. The election by the chapter, the confirmation by the archbishop, registration, consecration, restitution of the temporalities, parliamentary fees, homage and installation all brought heavy costs. A new seal had to be cut, episcopal arms issued and robes purchased. In addition, the first year's income (or 'first fruits') were payable to the Crown. Bishop Nicolson of Carlisle spent five hundred pounds in two months in 1702 on his entry to his diocese and Archbishop Sharp of York in 1691 paid nearly seven hundred pounds.[31] In addition, Sharp also had to pay fees for admission to the Privy Council which he did in 1702.[32] William Wake wrote a detailed account of his costs on his appointment to Lincoln diocese in 1705, which came to £598 8s 3d.

| | |
|---|---|
| Fees for Conge d' Elire | £56 11s 6d |
| Commendam fees | £49 7s 1d |
| Fees for Chapter Election | £19 2s 3d |
| Confirmation fees | £50 8s 8d |
| Doctors' Commons fees | £90 10s 0d |
| Consecration costs | £57 10s 0d |
| Homage fees | £113 7s 0d |
| Restitution of Temporalities | £69 10s 4d |
| Parliament fees | £10 8s 0d |
| Habit | £28 12s 0d |
| Other charges (seals etc) | £26 18s 3d |
| Composition fees and Installation | £25 10s 0d |
| Total | £598 8s 3d.[33] |

As a general rule, bishops had to borrow considerable amounts of money to cover these costs, and most took at least five years to clear the debt. For some bishops the debts they incurred during their appointments stayed with them for longer. Bishop Nicolson took seven years to repay his debts. In the eighteenth century about a quarter of all bishops never realised a profitable year from their tenure of a diocese.[34] Frederick Keppel, bishop of Exeter (1728–1777) died in 1777 and was said to have been 'immeasurably in debt', owing his tailor £1,000 and his brother

£5,000.[35] The Whig satirist Peter Pindar noted that Bishop John Ross of Exeter was so debt-ridden that he could not afford to receive George III at the palace when the king visited Exeter in August 1789.[36]

An additional problem was that the buildings of a diocese – especially episcopal palaces – were assessed for dilapidations at the end of an episcopate. A new bishop might have serious problems extracting money from his predecessor's widow or children to pay for such repairs. One of the examples already mentioned, Bishop Charles Trimnell, died a year after his translation from Norwich to Winchester diocese and this left his family with all the debts and none of the income from the post. When, in 1762, Richard Osbaldeston succeeded Thomas Hayter as bishop of London, he was obliged to seek £1,500 in dilapidations to restore Fulham Palace and other property to the condition in which they should have been left. These sums had to be paid from Bishop Hayter's estate.[37] When a diocese owned extensive properties, dilapidations could be crippling to a bishop's estate; the diocese of Winchester, with palaces in Winchester, Farnham and Chelsea, could be especially problematic. In 1761, on the death of Bishop Hoadly, his chaplain wondered whether his estate would bear the cost of 'two annuities, & one legacy, and his funeral charges and dilapidations of 3 vast houses.'[38]

The costs of maintaining palaces, especially when a diocese owned more than one, led some bishops to find some alternative use for them. In 1756 Bishop Hoadly allowed the palace at Winchester to be used as a barracks for Hessian troops who were mercenaries serving Britain in the Seven Years' War.[39] Archbishop William Wake of Canterbury arranged to lease the palace at Canterbury, which was in a poor state of repair, to a Mrs. Juxon. To Wake's dismay, Juxon sublet it to a company of actors in Lent 1715.[40] The poet Anna Seward occupied the palace at Lichfield from 1754 to 1809, during which time it became a centre of provincial literary culture attracting visitors that included Samuel Johnson and Erasmus Darwin.[41]

Despite their unjust reputation for neglect, eighteenth-century bishops spent huge sums repairing palaces and houses, and rebuilding whole swathes of episcopal properties.[42] Some bishops were exceptional builders. John Hough, bishop of Worcester (1751–1743) spent £7,000 on the three palaces in his diocese.[43] Between 1774 and 1776 Bishop John Thomas of Rochester spent £3,000 on renovating the bishop's palace at Bromley, and landscaped the park.[44] Edmund Keene built two palaces, the first when he was Bishop of Chester and the second when he was translated to Ely. Between 1754 and 1757, the red-brick palace on the Abbey Square at Chester was described by William Cole as follows:

> The Palace is now rebuilt from the Ground, consisting of 2 exceeding lofty & spacious Rooms, & other Apartments, all which the Bishop shewed to me, dining with him on Saturday Aug: 6 1757. when he told me had expended 2200 Pounds, near 3 years income of his Bishopric on it. At one End of the grand Salon is a very neat Library with Light only from above, thro' which the Bp has an opportunity to go to his private Chapel & to the Cathedral, without passing thro' any Court or yard.[45]

Later, as Bishop of Ely, Keene built the grand neo-classical London town-house at Ely House, Dover Street. It was designed by Sir Robert Taylor, to replace the ancient palace of Ely House at Holborn. It was such a huge building that Mary Yorke, wife of Bishop James Yorke of Ely, was quite intimidated by it.[46] Indeed the scale of some palaces were excessive. Bishop Auckland Castle, residence of the Bishops of Durham, consisted of fifty-nine rooms and possessions valued at over £2,400. In Worcester diocese, Hartlebury Castle consisted of sixty-four rooms and possessions costing over £1,200.[47]

Sometimes the scale of expenditure on buildings was daunting. Archbishop Thomas Herring found maintaining the palaces at Lambeth and Croydon a cause of anxiety, he wrote on 21 May 1748:

> The repair of these two old Palaces takes up too much of my Time & Thoughts & if I have not especial care, will prey too much upon my income too. I think, I shall make them extreamly pleasant, but yesterday at Croydon I was a little alarm'd for upon stripping the Roof of ye Great Hall in order for new Tyling, I found so many & so essential Decays, that I doubt, I must call in ye Expensive advices of Dr Flitcroft, ye great architect.[48]

One of the principal problems with buildings was that, as bishops grew older, their incentive to spend money on buildings that their families would never live in diminished. Bishop Beilby Porteus of London, as he got older, decided not to build a new library at Fulham Palace given his age, and Bishop Richard Watson of Llandaff, whose diocese lacked an episcopal residence at all, wrote that when it was likely that a bishop might be translated to another diocese there was a disincentive to restore their buildings.[49]

Even after the appointment and entry costs were cleared, the annual running costs of a bishop were very high. Bishops were expected to spend part of the year in London, attending parliament.[50] In the eighteenth century there were fewer than a hundred peers and twenty-six bishops with seats in the Lords, so bishops' votes were critical. Paying for a London house and travel to and from the diocese were costly. Some bishoprics owned London palaces including: Ely, Durham, Canterbury, and York, but other poorer sees did not. Bishop Thomas Watson of St David's in the 1690s was so reduced that he was obliged to live in a London inn when attending parliament, and some bishops were forced to rely on the hospitality of their fellow bishops or of temporal peers. Bishop Joseph Butler of Bristol was obliged to hire lodgings when he stayed in London.[51] One of the reasons why London canonries were attractive as *commendams* is that they gave bishops a place to live.

In addition to parliamentary business, all the responsibilities of the diocese came out of the bishop's income. In this sense there was no separation of personal from official income or expenditure. Visitation tours every three years, the costs of legal cases, the salaries of secretaries and chaplains all came from the bishop's own funds. The more active a bishop, the more costs he incurred and the greater the effect on his purse. Bishops found lawsuits especially difficult, since they were often protracted and might not be resolved during their tenure of the see. Bishop William Lloyd spent a huge sum pursuing his right to appoint to a parish in his diocese of St Asaph, going to the courts three times to defend his rights.[52]

Visitations were especially costly. They entailed the printing of visitation enquiries sent out to each parson and parish. These were returned and analysed; and during the visitation itself the bishop pursued issues that concerned him. The bishop often issued a printed charge to the clergy to draw attention to his practical or theological concerns. The bishop was usually accompanied by a chaplain, registrar and other officials, or their deputies. In addition to the transport costs of carriages and horses, there was accommodation to be covered as well as hospitality for the local clergy. Bishops took these duties seriously and most discharged them with considerable care and conscientiousness.[53] The cost of visitations ran usually to hundreds of pounds. During the eighteenth century there was a growing trend to separate visitations from confirmation tours, during which the bishop toured his diocese and confirmed people at local churches.[54] The effect of this trend was to double the time and costs of episcopal duties. And on occasion visitation led to extraordinary costs. Bishop Nicholas Claggett of St David's was obliged to replace a carriage since his was destroyed during a journey from Brecon to Abergwili in 1733.[55]

Expenditure by the bishops was much more predictable than income, but it was also diverse and not easily managed. At Salisbury, Hoadly estimated that wages for diocesan staff were fairly stable, though they extended to payments to maintain the bishop's stall in the cathedral and the salary of the master of the Cathedral School. The bishops also paid for the Salisbury charity-school boys' clothing, a widows' almshouse and to the fathers of the 'bishop's choristers'. The bishops of Salisbury were responsible for the salary of the city prison keeper including food for the prisoners at Christmas and for various payments for the High Bailiff and Steward of the Cathedral. Land and window taxes on episcopal properties were significant items, amounting in Salisbury to eighty-four pounds per annum. The episcopal property also paid poor rates, and this had to be paid to the separate parishes in which the property lay. Allowances had to be made for the refreshment and entertainment of tenants at rent payment days. The whole picture was complex and confusing and required a methodical and painstaking collector on whom the bishop could rely, but in the case of Salisbury this cost about ten percent of the income of the bishopric.[56]

Bishops were expected to make provision from their incomes for hospitality and charity. At their consecrations, bishops were enjoined to be hospitable to the poor and many had a distinguished record of doing so. The Bishops of Winchester, every day of the year, provided food for twenty-four poor men and women who came to the gates of their London house in Chelsea. The Archbishops of Canterbury were expected to do the same at Lambeth, Canterbury and Addington. It was only in the 1790s that the Archbishop of Canterbury ceased to provide charity to the poor at his gate. Previously, poor came to the gates of Lambeth Palace for small alms. This, Thomas Pennant claimed, was a 'happy change in the times', as it discouraged the 'idle poor' from begging and therefore encouraged industry.[57] Hospitality was not just expected by the poor. Archbishop William Dawes of York regularly invited the gentry and nobles of his diocese to dine 'to preserve an harmony and good understanding with his people' – by which he meant to promote the Tory interest in his diocese.[58] Hospitals particularly attracted episcopal patronage. Bishop Butler of Durham subscribed to the Newcastle Infirmary in 1751 and published a sermon for sale as a way of raising both interest and funds for the foundation. In the initial list of subscribers Butler's was the largest amount: £100 a year for five years and then £20 a year for life. He also left the infirmary £500 in his will.[59]

Bishops were also expected to contribute to the print culture of the period through the subscription to books. Clerical subscription to book publication was one of the main drivers of the development of the printing trade in the eighteenth century and many bishops were recorded as repeatedly subscribing money for the printing of important works of theology and scholarship. In the case of Welsh bishops, they were among the most consistent purchasers of books by subscription, and made remarkable financial sacrifices to keep Welsh book printing going.[60] In many cases, bishops published their own work, sermons or theological volumes, in aid of the poor or for particular charitable causes. Often these were ventures like the SPCK or missionary activity, but in some cases it was for the relief of poverty of episcopal children. Benjamin Hoadly in the 1750s re-issued some of his sermons specifically to raise income for the impoverished children of Bishop Gilbert Burnet.[61]

The purchase of books was also a major drain on episcopal incomes, and some bishops were noted bibliophiles. Bishop John Moore of Ely's library was one of the most distinguished in Europe, having taken years to assemble.[62] Richard Hurd's library at Worcester was so remarkable that he built his own library to house it.[63] Some libraries, like that at Lambeth, were so voluminous that they admitted members of the public if they sought to use them for scholarly purposes.

## 'Nolo Episcopari'

The problems that episcopal finances brought for the government was a recruitment crisis, which reached a head in the middle years of the century, especially in the 1740s. One of the motives for Thomas Herring's refusal of translation to Canterbury in 1747 was the financial burdens it would impose on him. He wrote to Lord Hardwicke:

> I am really poor. I am not ambitious of being rich, but have too much pride with, I hope, a small mixture of honesty to bear being in debt;

> I am now out of it and in possession of a clear independency of that sort. I must not go back and begin the world again at fifty-five.[64]

George Smalridge felt a similar concern in 1713 when he heard that he was to be offered a bishopric; it placed him 'under terrible apprehensions of a bishopric, the weight of which I have neither abilities of mind nor body nor purse to sustain.'[65] Similarly White Kennett, on receiving the nomination to Peterborough (which he accepted), anticipated only 'care, trouble, and want of money for the first two years at least'.[66] It was therefore entirely reasonable for clergy to express anxiety about the financial implications of accepting a bishopric. Daniel Waterland, for example, in 1738 declined the see of Llandaff because he was refused the chance of retaining the deanery of Wells (which had been promised to another cleric by the ministry) to help pay his expenses. John Egerton refused to accept Hereford in 1724 until he was also allowed to retain his rectory of Whitchurch, and in 1750 John Conybeare refused Bristol until he was allowed the deanery of Christ Church in addition.[67]

The offer of promotion for such men, though often attractive for the money, prestige and status it brought with it, was often met with a refusal. For example, the penniless Bishop Thomas Newton of Bristol declined the offer of the wealthy Primacy of Ireland in 1764.[68] In the 1747 case of Thomas Herring, mentioned earlier, the ministers refused to accept his decision and he was placed under enormous pressure to accept translation from York to Canterbury. The Duke of Newcastle told Herring that he simply could not refuse the offer as it would be a slur on the government that it could not persuade him, and two others, to accept the most senior appointment.[69] Lord Hardwicke resorted to begging Herring:

> For God's sake, for ye sake of ye King, ye country, and yr friends, don't decline. . . You are called by ye voice of ye King and of ye best intentioned men, and in this limited sense *vox populi est vox Dei*.[70]

Reluctantly Herring agreed to the move.

A year later, Newcastle sought a bishop for the diocese of Bangor. When Zachary Pearce refused it the Duke, together with Lord Hardwicke, placed great pressure on him. Hardwicke in exasperation asked Pearce: 'if clergymen of learning and merit will not accept the Bishoprics, how can the Ministers of State be blamed if they are forced to fill them with others less deserving?' It was an argument that struck home, and Pearce reversed his 'nolo'.[71]

## Conclusion

It seems that historians have misread the circumstances of the bishops of the eighteenth century. Far from rapaciously jostling for a mitre and being greedy for preferment, many bishops and clergy were wary of the financial dangers of appointment to the bench. In many cases clergy expressed anxiety that they were not just unworthy to become bishops but that they might damage their family's interests in doing so. Occasionally, a long-lived bishop might make a fortune from his diocese, but most of the episcopate found that their tenure, even of the richest sees, came with such obligations that they would be unlikely to establish fortunes.

Some bishops left large fortunes for the endowment of charities. Foremost among these was Nathaniel Crewe, bishop of Durham (1674–1721). Crewe came from an aristocratic family and in due course inherited a barony. When he died in 1721, he was exceptionally wealthy but used his wealth to endow charities at the University of Oxford, augment the incomes of Durham diocesan livings, and distribute alms to the poor. Indeed his charities were so extensive that an office was established at Bamburgh Castle to administer the various schemes. Buildings, paupers, shipwrecked sailors, schools and a range of other causes were supported by the bishop's estate. By 1850 the Crewe charities distributed £9,000 per annum.[72]

In the second half of the eighteenth century, when increasing numbers of aristocratic and wealthy bishops were appointed, in many cases such bishops subsidised the Church from their private incomes. This is especially the case for those bishops, like Richard Trevor and Shute Barrington at Durham and Richard Hurd at Worcester, who put up new buildings for their sees. As Edward Cressett wrote in 1748 to the Duke of Newcastle, when he was offered the poorest diocese, that of Llandaff: 'although the revenues of the see may not be very considerable, I think my private fortune cannot be better employed than in his majesty's service. . .'[73]

We need to correct our view of the grasping eighteenth-century bishop from the caricature of the preferment hunter to the clergyman haunted by the financial worries that a mitre brought with it. It has been assumed that safeguarding the estates of a bishopric and assuring the incumbent of a big income were in conflict. But this is not always the case. Thomas Herring, while Bishop of Bangor, wrote to his cousin of the death of Archbishop Lancelot Blackburne, one of the bishops with the worst reputation in the eighteenth century. Herring wrote that Blackburne left £50,000 or even £60,000, yet Bishopthorpe, the archbishop's palace, was 'left in y^e best Repairs possible, both House & Gardens, & its Revenues in y^e compleatest Order.'[74]

## Notes

1 G. F. A. Best, *Temporal Pillars, Queen Anne's Bounty and the Ecclesiastical Commissioners of the Church of England* (Cambridge, 1964), pp. 196–8. N. Sykes, *Church and State in England in the Eighteenth Century* (Cambridge, 1934), pp. 61–3.

2 Edward Carpenter explained that Sherlock received a large estate from both his father and brother and that this was the money that some claimed he had 'shamefully amassed' from the diocese of London. Sherlock left a comparatively modest sum to his widow with the residue of his estate bequeathed to his old Cambridge college and his nephew, the bishop of Ely. E. Carpenter, *Thomas Sherlock*, (London, 1936), p. 324.

3 H. Norwood, 'The Curious Will of Bishop Barrington of Durham', *Northern History*, vol. XXXIX, No 2, 2002.

4 This was a reference to the Book of Zachariah, chapter 11: verse 5. The print depicted Sherlock receiving a mitre full of coins from the devil. The print is now extremely rare. British Museum number: 1868,0808.13138.

5 W. Gibson, *Benjamin Hoadly, 1676–1761, Enlightenment Prelate* (Cambridge, 2004), p. 282.

6 Françoise Deconinck-Brossard, 'Richard Trevor (1707–1771)', in *Oxford Dictionary of National Biography*, Oxford, 2004 [hereafter ODNB].

7 Despite holding one of the richest dioceses, that of Durham, for some years, he left only £9,000 in his will. –University of Durham, Archives and Special Collections, SGD 35/14.

8 W. King, *Political and Literary Anecdotes of His Own Time* (London, 1818), p. 185.

9 W. Gibson 'John Conybeare' in *ODNB*, Archbishop Secker arranged for two volumes of sermons to be published by subscription for their benefit in 1757. As there were 4,600 subscribers, many of whom took more than one copy, the results must have been satisfactory. Nevertheless Secker was obliged to solicit a pension of £140 for Conybeare's dependants from the King. In fact, Thomas Secker commented that 'he was the loser by his bishopric, and hath by no means made a competent provision for his two children.' –British Library, Add. Mss., 32,858 f. 108.

10 Gibson, *Benjamin Hoadly, 1676–1761*, p. 282.

11 The same applied to parish clergy. Samuel Wesley, rector of Epworth in Lincolnshire, inherited the parish with an income of £200 a year but through gross mismanagement it fell to less than £90 within a few years. By 1705 he was more than £300 in debt and was imprisoned for non-payment of his debts.

12 G. F. A. Best referred to commendams as a means to keep bishops solvent in the eighteenth century. Best, *Temporal Pillars*, p. 197.

13 British Library, Add. Mss, 34,412, Auckland Correspondence, John Moore to Lord Eden, no date, f. 281. Auckland Correspondence

14 A.W. Rowden *The Primates of the Four Georges* (London 1916), p. 139

15 N. Sykes *Church and State in England in the Eighteenth Century* (Cambridge 1934), p. 359. Bishops Ewer and Shipley both tried hard to avoid lingering long in Welsh sees for the same reason, ibid, pp. 360–361.

16 A. Hartshorne (ed.), *The Memoirs of a Royal Chaplain 1729–1763* (London 1905), p. 129.

17 F. G. James *North Country Bishop* (New Haven, 1956), p. 92.

18 Huntington Library, San Marino, California, Huntingdon Mss, HM 692, Benson to Lord Huntingdon 14 July 1737. In the same letter, Benson apologised that he was unable to send Huntingdon any cheese.

19 Christ Church, Oxford, Wake Mss, Letters 20, f. 542, Hough to William Wake, 28 May 1718.

20 Swindon and Wiltshire Record Office, 'An Account of the Annual Revenue of the Bishoprick of Sarum, transcribed from Bishop Hoadly's account.' CC/Bishoprick/486/1

21 R. Nelson, *The Life of Bishop George Bull* (London, 1713), p. 430.

22 J. D. Davies 'Adam Ottley' (bap. 1655, d. 1723) *ODNB*.

23 National Library of Wales [hereafter NLW], Ottley Mss, 1420 & 532. Ottley's estate was so small that his bequest to his sisters was just ten pounds each and other amounts amounted to a few shillings: TNA, Adam Ottley's Will, PROB 11/594, fol. 114

24 E. White, *The Welsh Methodist Society, the Early Societies of South West Wales, 1737–1750* (Cardiff, 2020), p. 27.

25 NLW, Church in Wales Mss, SD/ERA/19 and 20.

26 W. Gibson, 'The Finances of the Diocese of St David's in the Eighteenth Century: The Reforms of Bishop Charles Moss 1766–73' in the *Journal of Welsh Ecclesiastical History*, vol 3, (1986), p. 53.

27 Gibson, 'The Finances of the Diocese of St David's in the Eighteenth Century' p. 55.

28 NLW, Lucas MSS, 2922–5.

29 Gibson, 'The Finances of the Diocese of St David's in the Eighteenth Century' p. 57.

30 D. R. Hirschberg 'A Social History of the Anglican Episcopate, 1660–1760' Michigan University PhD thesis 1976, p. 377.

31 C. Jones `The Political and Financial Costs of an Episcopal Appointment in the Early Eighteenth Century' in *The Huntington Library Quarterly* (1990), vol 53, no 2, pp. 119–120. 'First fruits' were almost always paid over a number of years, usually five, to enable the bishop to afford the expense.

32 Gloucestershire Archives, Lloyd-Baker Mss, John Sharp papers, D3549/6/4/29.

33 C. Jones 'The Political and Financial Costs of an Episcopal Appointment in the Early Eighteenth Century', pp. 119–120.

34 Hirschberg 'A Social History of the Anglican Episcopate, 1660–1760', pp. 399, 407.

35 W. P. Courtney, revised by William C. Lowe 'Frederick Keppel (1729–1777)', in *ODNB*.

36 P. Pindar, *The Works of Peter Pindar* (London, 1794), i, 284–5. Instead, Ross proposed that the King should stay with the Dean of Exeter.

37 British Library, Add MS 5831, William Cole's Collections, Vol. XXX, f. 52, I owe this reference to Daniel Reed.

38 Hartshorne (ed.), *The Memoirs of a Royal Chaplain 1729–1763*, p. 354. This contests claims that Hoadly was avaricious for which see R. Luckett 'Church and College, 1660–1745' in E. E. Rich (ed.) *St Catharine's College, Cambridge* (Cambridge, 1973), p. 136.

39 John Byng, *The Torrington Diaries* (London, 1935) i, p. 79.

40 N. Sykes, *William Wake: Archbishop of Canterbury, 1657–1737* (Cambridge, 1957), i, pp. 235–8.

41 M. Roberts, 'Close Encounters: Anna Seward, 1742–1809, A Woman in Provincial Cultural Life' University of Birmingham MLitt thesis, 2010, pp. 8–12.

42 M. Ashby, 'Episcopal Palaces in Georgian England: form, function and meaning' Cambridge University PhD thesis, 2015. Appendix two gives a list of major building works carried out in the eighteenth century.

43 J. Lock, 'John Hough (1651–1743) in *ODNB*.

44 N. Aston, 'John Thomas (1712–1793) in *ODNB*.

45 British Library, Add MS 5836, Cole notebooks, f. 219v.

46 Ashby 'Episcopal Palaces in Georgian England: form, function and meaning', pp. 134, 197.

47 Ashby 'Episcopal Palaces in Georgian England: form, function and meaning', p. 192.

48 University of Nottingham, Special Collections, Portland Manuscripts, PWV/120/56, Archbishop Thomas Herring to William Herring, May 21st 1748.

49 Beilby Porteus, *A Brief Account of Three Favourite Country Residences, to which is added Death, a Poetical Essay* (London, [1808]), p. 45; Richard Watson, *A Letter to His Grace the Archbishop of Canterbury* (London, 1783), p. 20. Contemporaries recognised that bishops with families might be disinclined to build. William Cole explained Thomas Gooch's architectural inactivity at Ely on the grounds that he had 'a family to succeed him'. British Library, Add MS 5828, Cole notebooks, f. 127. John Macky wrote in 1724: 'You must not expect to hear of great Magnificence in the *English* Bishops Palaces for as all their Improvements go to their succeeding Bishops, and not to their Families, they generally keep up the Conveniencies of their Predecessors, without making many Additions'. John Macky, *A Journey Through England in Familiar Letters* (London, 1724), ii, p. 11. I owe these references to Mike Ashby.

50 The bishop of Sodor and Man, as a member of the Tynwald, the Man legislature, did not sit in the House of Lords and therefore often did not spend time in London.

51 C. Cunliffe, 'Joseph Butler (1692–1752)' in *ODNB*.

52 D. R. Thomas, *A History of the Diocese of St Asaph* (Oswestry, 1908), i, pp. 128–9. At the same point, it should be said that in some dioceses there were customary perquisites, usually in the form of fees, payable to the bishop and other officials for acts and processes in the episcopal court.

53 Borthwick Institute of Historical Research, York, V. 1717–1719, Miscellaneous Items: A Plan for his Grace's Ordinary Visitation held in the Year 1719, I owe this to Daniel Reed.

54 P. Tovey, *Anglican Confirmation 1662–1820* (Farnham, 2014).

55 S. R. Thomas, 'The Diocese of St David's in the eighteenth century', MA thesis, University of Wales, 1983, p. 238.

56 Swindon and Wiltshire Record Office, 'An Account of the Annual Revenue of the Bishoprick of Sarum, transcribed from Bishop Hoadly's account.' CC/Bishoprick/486/1

57 T. Pennant, *Of London* (London, 1790), p. 20.

58 Hirschberg, 'A Social History of the Anglican Episcopate, 1660–1760', 396.

59 Cunliffe, 'Joseph Butler' in *ODNB*.

60 G. H. Jenkins, *Literature, Religion and Society in Wales 1660–1730* (Cardiff 1978), pp. 275–8.

61 Gibson, *Benjamin Hoadly, 1676–1761*, p. 279

62 J. Ringrose, 'The Royal Library: John Moore and his Books', in Peter Fox, ed., *Cambridge University Library: The Great Collections* (Cambridge, 1998), pp. 78–89.

63 C. Penney, 'A Bishop and His Books: Richard Hurd and his Library at Hartlebury Castle', *The Book Collector*, 60 (2011); C. Penney, 'Richard Hurd, Bishop and Bibliophile', *West Midlands History* (issue 3, winter 2013), pp. 34–6.

64 Rowden, *The Primates of the Four Georges*, p. 194.

65 HMC Portland, vol 5, p. 321.

66 G. V. Bennett, *White Kennett, 1660–1728* (London, 1957), p. 205. Exactly the same view was expressed by Bishop Lloyd of Norwich when he was offered translation to Gloucester – C. J. Abbey, *The English Church and its Bishops 1700–1800* (London, 1887), i, p. 168.

67 Hartshorne (ed.), *The Memoirs of a Royal Chaplain 1729–1763*, p. 70; Hirschberg, 'A Social History of the Anglican Episcopate, 1660–1760', p. 347.

68 Hartshorne (ed.), *The Memoirs of a Royal Chaplain 1729–1763*, p. 289. Abbey, *The English Church and its Bishops 1700–1800*, i, p. 138.

69 N. Sykes `Bishop Butler and the Church of His Age' *Durham University Journal*, vol 43, no 1 (1950), p. 5.

70 Rowden, *The Primates of the Four Georges*, pp. 193–5.

71 *The Lives of Dr Edward Pocock. . . Dr Zachary Pearce. . . Dr Thomas Newton. . . and the Revd Philip Skelton* (London, 1816), i, p. 399.

72 C. E. Whiting, *Nathaniel, Lord Crewe, Bishop of Durham 1674–1721* (London, 1940), pp. 328–30.

73 British Library, Newcastle Letters, Add. Mss, 32,717, f 528 23 December 1748.

74 University of Nottingham Special Collections, Pw, V 120, bound volume of letters from Thomas Herring, Archbishop of Canterbury to his cousin William Herring, Chancellor of York. Thomas Herring to William Herring, 9 April 1743. I owe this reference to Daniel Reed.

# THE ECONOMIC NETWORK OF AN EIGHTEENTH-CENTURY CLERGYMAN[1]

Jonas Lindström, Uppsala University

When Gustaf Berg in 1771 moved from his position as chaplain in Dalhem to become rector in the parish of Martebo, some 20 kilometres away, he arranged with three of his new parishioners that they would go to Dalhem and bring back some goods that he had left behind there. In return, the three parishioners were released from one day of their ploughing duty.[2]

During his time as a pastor on the Swedish isle of Gotland in the latter part of the eighteenth century, Gustaf Berg kept careful records of his economic transactions. The note about the arrangement is one of many thousand entries in an account book that ran over thirty years. These records point to an important but not well researched aspect of the relationship between the pastor and his parishioners: their day-to-day economic dealings with each other and their mutual economic dependency. The purpose of this article is to shed some light on this aspect by examining the economic transactions of the pastor and the web of social relationships in which they were a part.

The parish clergy were key figures in early modern Europe. They directed religious life in the community and acted as important links between the local sphere and the national society.[3] This makes them interesting objects of study not only in themselves, but because we can learn a lot about the wider society from their activities and relations. As this article shows, they could be important economic agents too. Economic ties as well as religious duties and social obligations bound the clergyman to the lives of his parishioners.

The empirical basis as well as the point of departure of this article is one account book of one Swedish minister. It goes without saying that it does not speak for every pastor in early modern Europe or Sweden. However, as Laurence Fontaine has argued, informal economic connections of the past are best apprehended through microstudies.[4] This article puts the account book in the larger context of the early modern

https://doi.org/10.16922/jrhlc.6.2.4

economy. It argues (1) that the pastor was part of an embedded economy based on credit, (2) that the pastor as a rent-owner had a very special position in this economy, and (3) that this position influenced his relationship with his parishioners. Gustaf Berg was a merchant, a banker and an employer. None of these capacities was separable from his role as minister.

## The Pastor and His Flock

The relationship between the pastor and his parishioners can been studied from many angles. The spiritual function, though central, is only one dimension. The minister's first mission was to teach and preach the Christian faith and to conduct ceremonies that marked vital events in the villagers' lives. During his forty-three years as a chaplain and a rector, Gustaf Berg preached 2194 times, wedded 86 couples, baptised 328 children and buried 273 people.[5] As Phillip Hoffman has observed, rites of this kind bound the clergyman to the villagers.[6] According to Göran Malmstedt, who has studied the relationship between church and peasantry in seventeenth-century Sweden, the execution of these duties was what mattered to the peasants. As long as the ceremonies were performed, they cared less about the quality of the performance or whether or not the pastor was involved in any worldly activities on the side.[7]

Cultural affinity or distance between pastor and parishioners is another aspect. It was more subject to change than the religious core. The eighteenth century was preceded by ecclesiastical reforms in both Protestant and Catholic Churches. While the lifestyle and appearance of the rural clergy had been very similar to the average villager in the sixteenth century, the reforms of the seventeenth century aimed at a cultural separation between pastor and his flock in dress, manners and education.[8] William Jacob has described the clergy in the eighteenth century as a distinctive occupational group that did not quite belong.[9] A large degree of self-reproduction is likely to have increased a distinct identity. More than forty per cent of the Swedish clergy in the eighteenth century were sons of clergymen, and almost sixty per cent of their wives came from clerical homes.[10] Gustaf Berg was himself the son of a rector in a parish not far from where he was to serve and he married twice to daughters of clergymen in the same region. He had spent two years at the University of Uppsala.[11] In this respect, he was rather typical of a Swedish clergyman in the eighteenth century.

A third aspect, much emphasized in Swedish historiography, is the role of the clergyman in local and state administration. The Reformation made Swedish ministers agents of the state. They were the eyes and voice of the national government. They kept records of the population and reported about the condition of their parish to central authorities.[12] They read government announcements from the pulpit.[13] They chaired the vestry and answered for the social control of the parishioners.[14] In effect, the administrative burden on Swedish pastors grew significantly during the eighteenth century, even to the point that Swedish historians have asked how they were able to meet all their obligations.[15] The pastor's role in between state and community also had the potential of making his position in village life difficult and disputed.[16]

This article highlights a fourth dimension: the economic relationships between the clergy and the members of the congregation. We should not look upon this as something separate from other aspects, but linked to them. C. Scott Dixon has argued for the import of clerical maintenance as crucial to the assimilation of the minister in the local community.[17] The parishioners were obliged to support their pastor. A Swedish rector had three main sources of revenue: the glebe – a piece of land allotted for the minister, the tithes paid by his parishioners and various fees in relation to baptisms, wedding, funerals et cetera. In addition, many parishioners were obliged to perform labour service.[18] This could cause conflicts to be sure, but as Jacob points out, it also created shared interests between pastor and parishioners and meant that the clergyman needed to be closely involved in local affairs.[19] Although the ecclesiastical reformers of the seventeenth century expressed dislike for engagement in trade and other worldly affairs, the nature of clerical maintenance inevitably drew pastors into the market.[20] The Swedish Church Ordinance of 1571 prohibited ministers to engage in markets, it is true, but only if more than necessary. Many Swedish clergymen depended on additional incomes.[21]

Because of his reliance on payments and labour of his parishioners, the economic position of the clergyman depended on good relationships and cooperation with the people around him.[22] In a general sense, this made him no different from everyone else in the early modern world. Social relationships and cooperation were crucial in what has been described as an embedded economy. The position of the pastor should be seen in this light.

## Scarcity, Credit and Embeddedness: Contours of an Early Modern Economy

In 1952, Swedish sociologist Börje Hanssen published a dissertation on socioeconomic relationships in early modern Sweden. One main argument of this now classic study is that economic relationships in the early modern period were never purely economic, but conflated with all sorts of social relationships.[23] According to Hanssen, scarcity was a key, or even defining, component of the early modern economy. Access to vital resources varied over the seasons, insufficient amounts of labour and tools in a single household necessitated cooperation and lending between neighbours, and lack of ready cash generated a barter economy based on credit and social relations.[24]

Hanssen seems not to have been aware of the writings of Karl Polanyi, whose *The Great Transformation* had been published eight years earlier and whose characterization of the early modern economy was very similar. They both stressed that economic behaviour understood as profit maximization is a modern phenomenon. Polanyi writes:

> The outstanding discovery of recent historical and anthropological research is that man's economy, as a rule, is submerged in his social relationships. He does not act so as to safeguard his individual interest in the possession of material goods; he acts so as to safeguard his social standing, his social claims, his social assets.[25]

Instead of motives of gain and distinct economic institutions, production and distribution were ensured by principles of reciprocity and redistribution.[26] Polanyi coined the term 'embeddedness' to account for the logic of this pre-modern, pre-capitalist economy. To him, and to Hanssen, the early modern economy represented a stage in historical development that was qualitatively different from the modern world, distinguished by another type of rationality.[27]

Scarcity, credit and embeddedness have remained key elements in descriptions of the early modern economy. Craig Muldrew has stressed that all households, from the wealthiest to the poorest, were entangled in webs of credit and obligations and Laurence Fontaine has maintained that credit relations lay at the heart of all social relationships in the early modern period.[28] Rather than two successive phases, however, historians today tend to see coexistence and overlap between an economy based on networks, trust and moral obligations, on the one side, and impersonal market transactions on the other. Because there were few formal credit institutions, credit relationships were personal and dependent on who lent and who borrowed.[29] Accordingly, recent research puts much emphasis on inequality, tension and power relations as integral aspects of embeddedness.

It has been suggested that credit was the result of a perpetual lack of ready cash.[30] Perhaps its roots ran deeper. James C. Scott has argued that the vulnerability of agrarian production – the constant risk of a failed harvest – generated a moral economy among peasants in which resources were redistributed from those who had to those who had not.[31] This should not be understood as pure charity. Generous behaviour of the better-off legitimized their position and could be converted into moral claims on goods and services.[32]

If Polanyi, Muldrew and others are right, then the local clergyman too was involved in a multitude of credit relationships and this cannot be separated from his position as a man of the Church. Social and economic roles were inseparable in early modern society and there was little distinction between the religious and the secular.[33] Merchants often wrote religious sentences on the cover or first pages of their account books.[34]

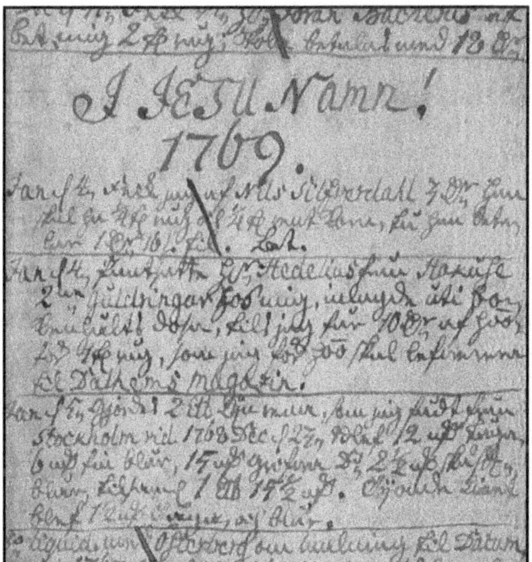


A page in the account book of Gustaf Berg.
(Photo: Benny Jacobsson)

Gustaf Berg started every new year in his account book with the words 'In the name of Jesus'.

## Gustaf Berg and His Account Book

Gustaf Berg was not the only Swedish pastor who kept a record of his private transactions. 150 years earlier, between 1623 and 1636, a rector in a Scanian parish noted his private dealings in a volume that otherwise was used for the church accounts. Hanssen used these accounts, which include more than 1600 entries, to map the economic network of the rector and to explore the characteristics of his economic dealings. He found, for example, that two-thirds of the transactions did not involve any money and that credit – both as explicit loans and as delayed payments – was crucial.[35]

Private accounts of this sort are rare, but do exist. An exceptional case, in Sweden at least, is the archive left by three generations of rectors who lived and served in different parishes on the isle of Gotland.[36] Gustaf Berg belonged to the second generation. He was born the son of a rector in 1727. When his older stepbrother was appointed rector in the neighbouring parish of Dalhem in 1753, Berg followed him there to serve as his assistant. A few years later Berg was appointed chaplain in Dalhem. In 1771, at the age of forty-four, he was promoted to rector in the parish of Martebo. Berg stayed and served in Martebo until his death in 1798.[37]

Berg died a relatively wealthy man.[38] The sheer number of objects listed in his probate inventory makes this evident. Among his possession were, for examples, fifty-two silver spoons in addition to twenty-two other silver objects, three mirrors, eleven pairs of linen curtains, twelve horses, eight oxen and eighteen cows.[39] There were twelve beds in the rectory, which were probably needed as the size of the household size oscillated between twelve and sixteen people.[40] Apart from the glebe, he and his wife owned a freehold farm.[41]

Berg started on his account book in 1768 and kept it for thirty years until his death. The first entry on the first page reads:

> 1768 Jan 9. Johan Sysne received ¾ barrel of pure barley at 4 *daler* 16 *öre*. So now he owes me 24 *öre*. *Vid.* [see] 1767 Jan 14 & Sept 4. *Vid.* August 31.[42]

The entry immediately shows a number of things. First, it was the continuation of an older account book as it referred to notations from the previous year. Second, the transaction with Johan Sysne, a peasant who lived twenty-five kilometres from Dalhem, was part of a long-term credit relationship. Third, even if everything was given a monetary value, it was not necessarily – in fact, it seldom was – ready cash that changed hands.[43] When the debt was cleared in August, Berg received fish from Johan Sysne.[44]

Based on Berg's entries, the following sections examine the character of his connections. After a general overview of the network, pointing to three different kinds of economic relationships, I look more deeply into the nature of the credit relations and discuss their impact on the relationship between pastor and parishioners.

## The Spatial and Social Structure of the Network

A geographical analysis of Gustaf Berg's economic network, based on the entries in his account book in two time periods – the first two years of the accounts, from January 1768 to December 1769, and the first two years after Berg's move to Martebo, where he became rector, that is, from May 1771 to April 1773 – displays two fundamental traits of Berg's economy. First, it was a local, or perhaps regional, economy. Apart from two outliers – Stockholm and Borås – and two households from the neighbouring island of Öland, all connections lived on Gotland. When Berg bought things from Stockholm, his affairs were mediated through relatives and other people from Gotland. Borås was a town in the western part of Sweden, whose inhabitants had a special privilege to travel around the country to sell textiles.[45] This is why they turn up in Berg's account book.

Second, when Berg moved from Dalhem to Martebo and began to serve as rector in the latter parish, he immediately started to trade with his new parishioners while at the same time retaining very few economic connections in his former home area. About half of Berg's economic connections lived in his home parish in both periods. Another indication of his swift assimilation into a new economic environment is that seventy-five per cent of the household heads who were listed in the 1771 poll tax list of the parish had turned up in Berg's accounts after only three years.[46] The short time in which new connections and new credit relations were established after the move to Martebo suggests that it was expected of him that he would trade with the people in his surroundings. In turn, this suggests that his predecessor had a similar role.

Figure 1 shows the proportions of different social groups – counted by number of individual households – in the account book. As a chaplain and a rector, Gustaf Berg had contacts with all sorts of people. The social extensiveness of his network is visible also in his economic affairs. Berg's transactions involved both lodgers and a bishop and everyone in between. Peasants made up about forty-five per cent of the households both before and after the move to Martebo and persons of rank about one sixth. The increase in the proportion of landless among Berg's connections after his move to Martebo, from fourteen to twenty per cent, is probably explained by a larger landless population in the latter area. Thus, although most of the specific individuals Berg traded with changed upon his move to Martebo, the social composition of his economic network was altered very little.

There was almost an inverted relationship between geographical distance and social distance. Remote connections were generally with merchants and other persons of rank. Lodgers, on the other hand, being on the opposite end of the social ladder, all lived in the vicinity. Landed peasants and artisans, who were somewhere in between, lived both close and more far away.

Although Gustaf Berg's economic network involved all parts of society, a good many of his transactions were based on kin relations. Through his siblings and his wives, Berg was connected to many clergymen and civil servants on the isle of Gotland. This can be seen also in his economic transactions. In 1768–9, almost one fourth of the entries involved

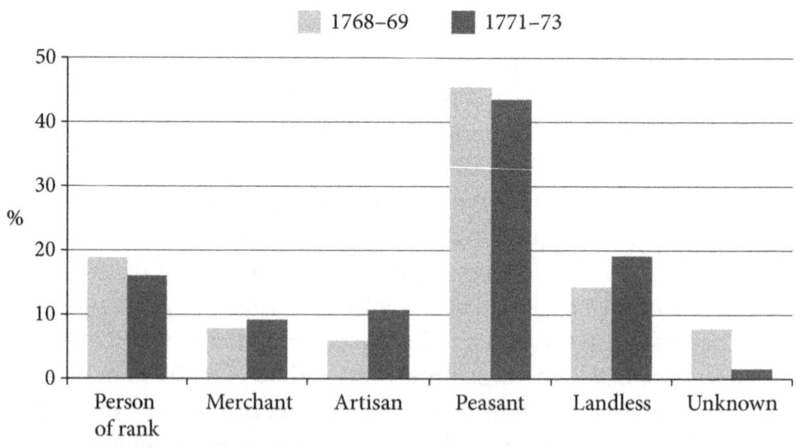


Figure 1. Social groups in Berg's account book, 1768–9 and 1771–3

relatives. Berg's most important economic contact in Visby, the only town on Gotland, was his brother. They constantly exchanged goods, money and services; in both 1768–9 and 1771–3, the brother appears once every second month in the accounts and his son-in-law appears just as often. Relatives both bought and sold goods on behalf of Berg. When a brother-in-law visited in Stockholm, he helped Berg to order some brass objects, and when a sister visited an auction, she bought a clock for him.[47] The bishop from whom Berg bought newspapers in 1796 was the brother of Berg's late wife.[48] Berg's kin relations certainly widened his economic field of action and facilitated many transactions.

In conclusion, the accounts give evidence of three kinds of economic relationships:

1. When it comes to exchanges with kin and peers, that is, people of equal social standing, Berg probably knew them well. In the accounts, Berg often called them 'Brother' or 'Sister', even when they were more distant relatives or not relatives at all. Their economic transactions were probably only a small part of their dealings with each other.
2. Exchanges with merchant and artisans, many of whom lived in Visby, might have been more purely economic. Berg bought or sold certain goods in return for money and/or other goods. Some artisans and some merchants reappear in the accounts, but their relationships to Berg need not to have been anything more than this. Perhaps some of the more distant peasants, who visited Berg to buy grain or sell fish, belonged to this category.
3. Berg's relationships with the peasant and landless population of his home parish were different. Compared to the previous group, they had a more permanent and more multifaceted relationship with him, but of a very different kind than the first group. Not only was he their social superior in religious and communal errands, but apart from credit relations, though also intertwined with them, he had economic claims on them.

I will return to group three, after first looking upon the credit relationships in more detail.

## An Economy Based on Credit

Muldrew has claimed that almost all buying and selling in the early modern period involved some form of credit.[49] The accounts of Gustaf Berg confirm this view. Berg constantly owed people and people was constantly indebted to him. Most entries in the account books are crossed over, symbolising the clearance of a debt. Soon after one debt had been cleared, however, a new debt was usually created.

The account book also confirms the image of an exchange economy in which the use of money was limited. Very few of the transactions that Berg recorded in his notebook consisted of immediate monetary payments for a product or a service. Much more often, a product (e.g. grain) was exchanged for another product (e.g. fish) or some kind of service. Payments were frequently delayed and piecemeal. For example, in January 1768 a peasant received two loads of straw from Berg. One load was paid for immediately with a load of timber. The other half was to be paid in butter. This second half of the payment was then divided into two parts and the peasant came to deliver shares of the agreed amount of butter on two different occasions.[50]

Money was not non-existent, however. Both small coins and larger bills changed hands. A civil servant, whom Berg met on the road and who apparently was short of coins, borrowed the small amount of six *öre* (*c.* 0.2 *daler*) from him, while a rector borrowed one thousand *daler* in cash.[51] Many times, payment consisted partly of money, partly of goods. When Berg bought a mirror at a price of forty-five *daler*, he paid twenty-five *daler* in cash and one barrel of rye valued at ten *daler*. The remaining ten *daler* were paid more than a year later with another barrel of grain.[52] Shortage of money probably explains some of the reliance on credit and on goods and services as means of payment, but it was not the single cause. Even when money was at hand it was not always the preferred means of payment. A shoemaker who visited Berg in June 1798 to make shoes for him explicitly did not want money but preferred to be paid the following winter in grain and straw.[53]

Hanssen has made a distinction between loans based on trust and formal credit, which involved interest, written documentation and pledges. Whereas the former kind dominated among equals who knew each other well, the latter was generally between people from different social strata and milieus. With time, most noticeably during the nineteenth century, formal credit replaced loans based on trust even among equals.[54] According to Polanyi, this was a crucial step in the unembeddedness of the economy, that is, the historical development from a world in which all transactions were intertwined with personal relationships to a world of formal and impersonal transactions. In the case of Gustaf Berg, his account book might in itself be looked upon as a form of written documentation of credit relations. He had a certain drawer in one of his desks where he kept receipts and bonds. Yet, receipts, pledges and interest are mentioned only seldom in the accounts. When they appear, they involve siblings as well as neighbours and people who lived far away, sums are both small and large, and they exist in both 1768 and 1798. Thus, it is difficult to discern any clear pattern of when credit was formalized and when it was not. Money was mostly involved in transactions with people of a similar social standing, however, like other clergy, civil servants and merchants. Peasants most often paid with other goods (e.g. fish), but also by providing services, many times transport. Landless people often paid by doing labour.

### An Unequal Relationship

Credit was ubiquitous in early modern societies. Most people were indebted and most people had claims. In this sense, Gustaf Berg was no different from his parishioners. Yet, his position in this web of mutual dependencies differed markedly from those around him. The reciprocity of many of his credit relationships was intertwined with a more unequal form of redistribution in early modern society: the feudal rent.

Swedish pastors had certain rights in relation to their parishioners. First, they claimed a part, officially a tenth, of their produce in grain, hay, fish and livestock. While in the rest of Sweden after the Reformation two-thirds of the tithe was paid to the state and one-third to the rector, the local clergy of Gotland kept the entire tithe, partly because of custom, partly because of small and allegedly poor parishes.[55] Second, pastors had a claim on their parishioners' labour. The members of the congregation were obligated to build and repair the rectory buildings, but could also be required to do day labour for the pastor. Regional and even local differences were large in this respect.[56] In Gotland, the labour demand on parishioners was relatively far-reaching.[57] Third, parishioners paid fees to the clergyman on the occasion of baptisms, marriages, burials and other ceremonies, the sizes of which varied with the social and economic position of the payer.[58]

Although Berg kept separate accounts of these payments, they turn up in the present account book as well, because they were part and parcel of the same web of economic obligations. The claims could be traded for something else. In the beginning of this article I gave an example of three peasants who delivered goods instead of doing their ploughing duty. At other occasions, parishioners bought grain or hay from Berg simply by keeping what they would otherwise have paid him in tithe, offering instead money, services or other goods as payment.[59]

In April 1775, Berg and the lodger Fredrik Nilsson settled their debts. Fredrik and his wife Anna Larsdotter appear frequently in the account book. Anna regularly spun yarn for the rector and Fredrik fished, among other things, mostly in return for grain. This time, both of them had done day labour for Berg. He had worked for six days and she four-and-a-half. She had, moreover, spun yarn. Together, they had earned almost three *daler*. One-quarter of their earnings was applied to clear the cost of their child's funeral. In effect, Fredrik and Anna paid for the funeral with their labour.[60]

The tithe gave Berg the upper hand against his trading partners by providing him with a substantial surplus of grain, arguably the most important product in the early modern economy. Grain was, by far, the type of goods that he most commonly sold or lent. Some of this grain Berg produced himself; like most Swedish pastors, he was also a farmer. Besides the glebe, he owned two successive freeholdings (one in Dalhem and one in Martebo). Tithe collection explains most of his large surplus of grain, though, and because of this surplus, Berg was able to keep a large stock of grain that could be sold (or lent) to the people of his parish as well as to townspeople.

Most of the grain was sold in the first months of the year, when the harvest had been threshed and the tithe had been collected. At times, Berg sold large quantities to merchants in Visby.[61] Much more common were smaller purchases that consisted of one barrel or less.[62] Although they were mostly carried out in the winter too, small purchases occurred all year round. Thus, Berg had enough surplus to be able to sell also when other households ran short or when the demand was particularly high, for example in sowing seasons. In an economy characterized by scarcity and seasonal variation, this gave him a significant advantage in relation to his parishioners.

## The Parsonage as an Open House

The most salient feature of Berg's accounts is the interconnectedness between his household economy and those of the households around him. The dependency was mutual – they needed him and he needed them – even though the relationships were not always equal. Early modern households were far from the discrete and closed units as which they have sometimes been depicted. Peter Laslett has remarked that as far back as the written evidence goes, Europe has never witnessed a 'natural economy', in which each family produced what they needed to survive.[63] This is obviously true of land-poor households, which lacked the necessary means of their subsistence and, therefore, were compelled to engage with the outside world.[64] It was no less true of the rich, because their large incomes and estates were dependent on the labour of others. The market has been an integrated part of the peasant economy at least since the Middle Ages.[65] Research on everyday work practices in the early modern era has shown that the household was just one of many frameworks for organizing work. Co-operation between neighbours and work in large-scale organizations were not detached from household production, however, but intertwined with it.[66] Joachim Eibach has suggested the concept the 'open house' to account for this permeable and flexible nature of household organization. Rather than closed and self-contained units, early modern households were entities open to a variety of social and economic activities.[67]

The parsonage was indeed an open house, in a number of ways. It was not only the liability of the clerical household, but of the entire parish. The rectory often hosted short-term and long-term guests, both rich and poor. It usually employed a large number of servants who moved in and out of the household. During Gustaf Berg's time as rector, between six and nine servants – on average, three male servants and four females – were living in his household.[68] There were also casual workers who stayed at the rectory for shorter periods of time.[69] The rectory has been described as the municipal hall of the time, whereto people came for marriage counselling as well as to get certificates of various kinds.[70] Perhaps the description of Gustaf Berg in the obituary as 'a Father of his parishes', to whom people often came for advice, may not have been a total exaggeration.[71] At least, we know from his accounts that Berg helped with, and was paid for, drawing up inventories, wills and petitions for people in the vicinity.[72]

Both parishioners and persons from further away came to Berg not only for services or advice, but also for goods. The large stock of hay and grain at the parsonage functioned as a reserve for the entire locality. To many lodgers in the parish, who had no or very little land of their own, the possibility of going to the rectory to buy grain was obviously a regular and essential part of the way they maintained themselves. But landholding households too could rely on the pastor to relieve temporary shortages. In July 1769, for example, Berg lent wheat and flour to several households on the condition that the loan was paid back as soon as they had harvested.[73] The transactions were not examples of redistribution in the traditional sense, because many times it was the parishioners themselves who had produced the products they bought back.

Berg too relied on his neighbours. Just after his move to Martebo, two of his new parishioners – two persons of rank – equipped him with seed and a ploughing team, respectively.[74] Another parishioner, a peasant, was paid to make a sofa for his new home.[75] The many servants who lived and served in the rectory formed a significant workforce, but in fact, the work that was needed to maintain the parsonage and the clerical family was distributed over a much wider range of people. On top of the labour service they owed to the rector, people were paid to thresh, clear land, transport goods, make furniture and clothes, etc.

Some parishioners turn up more frequently in the accounts and seem to have been particularly integrated in the economy of the pastor's household. In Dalhem lived a lodger called Årent Hansson. Berg called him an 'old man' (*gubbe*) in the accounts (he was about sixty years old).[76] In February 1768, he received some straw from Berg. In return, his wife Annika promised to spin yarn for him, something she did regularly. Årent, on his side, threshed and chopped wood. In addition to this, the couple leased a cow from Berg and paid for it by doing day labour.[77] After Berg had moved to Martebo, other lodger families took a similar role. The symbiosis and constant exchanges of labour, goods and money between these lodger households and the pastor are comparable with what has been described elsewhere in early modern Europe, where elite households provided poorer neighbours with key assets that they lacked in return for their labour.[78]

Credit was imperative in a society where many people had a difficult time making ends meet whilst institutional poor relief was far from sufficient.[79] At the same time, it created dependencies and tied workers to the creditor.[80] In effect, the total amount of labour Berg had access to and could control was much larger the what was provided by his own household, not only because of the labour services of the parishioners, but also because of a much wider web of credit relationships.

Jacob has found examples of British clergymen who acted as banker for their parishioners, but comments that they had this in common with many of their better-off neighbours.[81] This is true, but the pastor was not just any creditor because his lending activities were interlinked with his position as preacher and rent-owner. Economic relations were embedded not only in social relations of trust and cooperation, but of power and inequality, as well.

## Conclusion

The relationship between pastor and his parishioners was multi-layered. Not only was he their religious leader and representative of secular authorities, but he was also deeply involved in their economic affairs. The core of this economic position was the combination of his being a feudal rent-owner and the economic system being based on scarcity and credit.

Scott Dixon has argued that the success of a Lutheran clergyman after the Reformation depended on his ability to penetrate the web of social relations in the local community.[82] The same probably remained true in the eighteenth century. As a teacher and a preacher, a civil servant and local rent-owner, the pastor needed, above all, people to listen to him. His position in village life was not always easy. In seventeenth-century Sweden, peasants could literally lock the minister out of the church when he did not please them.[83] The economic demands of the clergy were a constant source of complaints.[84] New administrative tasks in the eighteenth century, many of which meant an increasing degree of surveillance, added to the structural opposition that existed between the pastor and the members of his congregation. Under these circumstances, the personal authority of the clergyman was key. By being a banker as well as a merchant and an employer, Gustaf Berg truly permeated the daily lives of his parishioners. People relied on him for their material well-being as well as for the blessedness of their souls. They came to him not only for his official services or fatherly advice, but also to buy or sell goods, offer him work or borrow money. This may have resulted in goodwill and veneration, but could just as well create bonds of coercion. In either case, it strengthened the relative position of the pastor in relation to his flock.

In a world where economic activities were embedded in social relationships, the economic affairs of the pastor may have been looked upon by both himself and the people around him as just another part of the pastoral care that was expected of him. It was not simply about charity – debts were almost never remitted – but about meeting social and economic obligations. In the end, it was about upholding a position of power.[85]

I do not claim that Gustaf Berg was representative. The sheer volume of written documentation left by him and his family is rather indicative of the opposite.[86] The special privileges of the clergy of Gotland by which they, unlike other Swedish pastors, kept the entire tithe themselves, created a different proportion between his pile of grain and the funds of the people around him. In relation to other Swedish clergymen he was quite wealthy. But given the general character of the early modern economy as well as the claims of the clergy on the products and labour of their parishioners, it is likely that many eighteenth-century clergymen in Europe had a similar role in the local economy.

## Notes

1 The author would like to thank Benny Jacobsson, who identified the source material, and Jessica Karlsson, who transcribed it.

2 Regional state archive in Visby (Landsarkivet i Visby, hereafter ViLA), Private accounts, 12 July 1771, Martin Gustafsons arkiv (hereafter MGA) F IV:77. According to the privileges of the clergy of Gotland, every peasant was obliged to do two ploughing days per year, one in the spring and one in the autumn. H. Levin. 'Bidrag till Visby stifts historia III: Införandet av svenskt kyrkoskick på Gotland efter freden i Brömsebro' in *Kyrkohistorisk årsskrift*, vol 11 (1910), p. 111.

3 C. Bergström, *Lantprästen: Prästens funktion i det agrara samhället 1720–1800: Oland-Frösåkers kontrakt av ärkestiftet* (Stockholm, 1991); W.M. Jacob, *The Clerical Profession in the Long Eighteenth Century, 1680–1840* (Oxford, 2007); C. Scott Dixon & L. Schorn-Schütte (eds), *The Protestant Clergy of Early Modern Europe* (New York, 2003); T. Tackett, *Priest and Parish in Eighteenth-Century France* (Princeton, 1977).

4 L. Fontaine, *The Moral Economy: Poverty, Credit, and Trust in Early Modern Europe* (New York, 2014), p. 6.

5 ViLA, Obituary of Gustaf Berg 18 September 1798, Martebo kyrkoarkiv C I:2, p. 106.

6 P. T. Hoffman, *Church and Community in the Diocese of Lyon 1500–1789* (New Haven, 1984), p. 53.

7 G. Malmstedt, *Bondetro och kyrkoro: Religiös mentalitet i stormaktstidens Sverige* (Lund, 2002), p. 125.

8 Hoffman, *Church and Community*: Malmström, *Bondetro och kyrkoro*, pp. 88–124; Tackett, *Priest and Parish*, pp. 154–5.

9 Jacob, *The Clerical Profession*, p. 305.

10 S. Carlsson, *Ståndssamhälle och ståndspersoner 1700–1865: Studier rörande det svenska ståndssamhällets upplösning*, 2nd ed. (Lund, 1973), pp. 202–3.

11 ViLA, Obituary of Gustaf Berg 18 September 1798, Martebo kyrkoarkiv C I:2, pp. 106–7.

12 P. Sköld, 'The Birth of Population Statistics in Sweden', in *The History of the Family*, vol 9, no 1 (2004).

13 E. Reuterswärd, *Ett massmedium för folket: Studier i de allmänna kungörelsernas funktion i 1700-talets samhälle* (Lund, 2001).

14 B. Furuhagen, *Berusade bönder och bråkiga båtsmän: Social kontroll vid sockenstämmor och ting under 1700-talet* (Stockholm, 1996).

15 Bergström, *Lantprästen*, p. 115; H. Enefalk, *Svenskarna och deras kyrkor* (Stockholm, 2017), p. 172–3.

16 Bergström, *Lantprästen*, p. 1; J. Goodale, 'The Clergyman between the Culture of State and Parish: Contestation and Compromise in Reformation Society', in C. Scott Dixon & L. Schorn-Schütte (eds), *The Protestant Clergy of Early Modern Europe* (New York, 2003).

17 Scott Dixon, *Reformation and Rural Society*, p. 83.

18 E. Gräslund Berg, *Till prästens bruk och nytta: Jord till prästgårdar i Sverige under medeltid och tidigmodern tid* (Stockholm, 2004), pp. 22–3; E. Sandstedt, *Prästerskapets ekonomiska och sociala villkor i Lunds stift 1723–1832* (Lund, 1986), pp. 29–94.

19 Jacob, *The Clerical Profession*, pp. 137–44.

20 Tackett, *Priest and Parish*, p 132.

21 Malmström, *Bondetro och kyrkoro*, p. 92.

22 Jacob, *The Clerical Profession*, pp. 137; Scott Dixon, *Reformation and Rural Society*, p. 86.

23 B. Hanssen, *Österlen: Allmoge, köpstafolk & kultursammanhang vid slutet av 1700-talet i sydöstra Skåne*. 2nd ed. (Stockholm, 1977 [1952]). p. 46.

24 Hanssen, *Österlen*, pp. 40–8.

25 K. Polanyi, *The Great Transformation: The Political and Economic Origins of Our Time* (Boston, 2001 [1944]), p. 48.

26 K. Polanyi, *The Great Transformation*, pp. 49–50.

27 D.C. North, 'Markets and Other Allocation Systems in History: The Challenge of Karl Polanyi' in *Journal of European Economic History*, vol 6 no 3 (1977).

28 C. Muldrew, *The Economy of Obligation: The Culture of Credit and Social Relations in Early Modern England* (Basingstoke, 1998), p. 95; Fontaine, *Moral Economy*.

29 C. H. Crowston, *Credit, Fashion, Sex: Economies of Regard in Old Regime France* (Durham, 2013), p. 98.

30 R. Ago, 'Using Things as Money: An Example from Late Renaissance Rome' in L. Fontaine (ed.) *Alternative Exchanges: Second-Hand Circulations from the Sixteenth Century to the Present* (New York, 2008), p. 43.

31 J. C. Scott, *The Moral Economy of the Peasants: Rebellion and Subsistence in Southeast Asia* (New Haven, 1976), pp. 2–5; P. Henningsen, 'Peasant Society and the Perception of a Moral Economy: Redistribution and Risk Aversion in Traditional Peasant Culture', in *Scandinavian Journal of History*, vol 26 no 4 (2001).

32 Scott, *Moral Economy*, pp. 41–2.

33 Jacob, *The Clerical Profession*, p. 9.

34 A. Grandell, *Äldre redovisningsformer i Finland* (Helsinki, 1944), p. 180.

35 Hanssen, *Österlen*, pp. 39–47.

36 In total, the family archive contains 33 volumes of private accounts from three generations of rectors from the 1720s to the 1840s, thus spanning 120 years.

37 O. Lemke, *Visby stifts herdaminne: Efter mestadels otryckta källor* (Örebro, 1892), pp. 126, 208–9, 217.

38 The net value of Berg's probate inventory was 2,519 *Riksdaler specie*. ViLA, Probate inventory of Gustaf Berg 26 November 1798, Gotlands norra häradsrätts arkiv F 2 A:67, no 3023. If deflated to regional rye prices, the sum can be compared to the Scanian rectors studied by Sandstedt. Counted in this way, Berg's net value was about four times larger than the average Scanian rector in the decades around 1800. Sandstedt, *Prästerskapets ekonomiska och sociala villkor*, p. 137. Rye prices from L. Jörberg, *A History of Prices in Sweden 1732–1914*,

*Vol. 1: Sources, methods, tables* (Lund, 1972), p. 133–7. See also ongoing PhD project by Beverly Tjerngren, Uppsala University, on social identity, social reproduction, and social mobility among Swedish parish rectors, 1700–1800.

39 ViLA, Probate inventory of Gustaf Berg 26 November 1798, Gotlands norra häradsrätts arkiv F 2 A:67, no 3023.

40 Swedish National Archive (Riksarkivet, RA), Poll tax registers 1771–1798, Mantalslängder 1642–1820 Gotlands län.

41 ViLA, Probate inventory of Märta Berg 18 June 1792, Gotlands norra häradsrätts arkiv F 2 B:3, no 25.

42 ViLA, Private accounts, 9 January 1768, MGA F IV:77.

43 C.f. Muldrew, *Economy of Obligation*, p. 101.

44 ViLA, Private accounts, 30 August 1768, MGA F IV:77.

45 P. Lundqvist, *Marknad på väg: Den västgötska gårdfarihandeln 1790–1864* (Göteborg, 2008).

46 RA, Poll tax registers 1771, Mantalslängder 1642–1820 Gotlands län.

47 ViLA, Private accounts, 29 July 1768, 10 January 1769, MGA F IV:77.

48 ViLA, Private accounts, 4 November 1797, MGA F IV:77.

49 Muldrew, *Economy of Obligation*, p. 95.

50 ViLA, Private accounts, 21 January 1768, MGA F IV:77.

51 ViLA, Private accounts, 19 July 1769, 22 May 1797, MGA F IV:77.

52 ViLA, Private accounts, 28 August 1769 MGA F IV:77.

53 ViLA, Private accounts, 19 July 1798, MGA F IV:77.

54 Hanssen, *Österlen*, pp. 40–4.

55 H. Levin, 'Bidrag till Visby stifts historia I. Den kyrkliga indelningen och prästrättigheterna på Gotland (Historik)', in *Kyrkohistorisk tidskrift*, vol 3 (1902), p. 199.

56 Sandstedt, *Prästerskapets ekonomiska och sociala villkor*, p. 89.

57 Levin, 'Bidrag till Visby stifts historia III', pp. 110–11.

58 Sandstedt, *Prästerskapets ekonomiska och sociala villkor*, pp. 79–84.

59 E.g. ViLA, Private accounts, 5 August 1771, 6 July 1773, 8 January 1787, MGA F IV:77.

60 ViLA, Private accounts, 3 April 1775, MGA F IV:77.

61 E.g. ViLA, Private accounts, 17 February 1768, 26 April 1778, MGA F IV:77.

62 Early modern data on grain consumption of an adult vary between three and six barrels per year. G. Hansson, *Såld spannmål av kyrkotionden: Priser i Östergötland under Sveriges stormaktstid* (Umeå, 2006), pp. 87–8.

63 P. Laslett, 'Family and Household as Work Group and Kin Group: Areas of Traditional Europe Compared', in R. Wall (ed.), *Family Forms in Historic Europe* (Cambridge, 1983), p. 539.

64 A. Knotter, 'Problems of the "Family Economy": Peasant Economy, Domestic Production and Labour Markets in Pre-Industrial Europe' in M. Prak (ed.), *Early Modern Capitalism: Economic and Social Change in Europe 1400–1800* (London, 2001).

65 A. Panjek., J. Larsson & L. Mocarelli (eds), *Integrated Peasant Economy in a Comparative Perspective: Alps, Scandinavia and Beyond* (Koper, 2017); S. Ghosh, 'Rural Economies and Transitions to Capitalism: Germany and England Compared (*c.*1200–*c.*1800')', in *Journal of Agrarian Change*, vol 16, no 2 (2016).

66 D. Lindström, R. Fiebranz, J. Lindström, J. Mispelaere & G. Rydén, 'Working Together', in M. Ågren (ed.), *Making a Living, Making a Difference: Gender and Work in Early Modern European Society* (New York, 2017); J. Lindström & J. Mispelaere, 'Interdependent Living: Labouring Families and the Swedish Mining Industry in the Late Seventeenth Century', The *History of the Family*, vol 22, no 1 (2017).

67 J. Eibach, 'Das offene Haus: Kommunikative Praxis im sozialen Nahraum der europäischen Frühen Neuzeit', in *Zeitschrift für Historische Forschung*, vol 38, no 4 (2011).

68 RA, Poll tax registers 1771–1798, Mantalslängder 1642–1820 Gotlands län.

69 E.g ViLA, Private accounts, 2 February 1793, MGA F IV:77.

70 Bergström, *Lantprästen*, pp. 21–2.

71 ViLA, Obituary of Gustaf Berg 18 September 1798, Martebo kyrkoarkiv C I:2, p. 107.

72 E.g. ViLA, Private accounts, 14 February 1769, 23 November 1794, 19 November 1797, MGA F IV:77.

73 ViLA, Private accounts, 19 July 1769, MGA F IV:77.

74 ViLA, Private accounts, 8 May 1771 MGA F IV:77.

75 ViLA, Private accounts, 1 May 1771, MGA F IV:77.

76 ViLA, Catechetical examination register 1750–1780, Dalhems kyrkoarkiv A I:1, p. 94.

77 ViLA, Private accounts, 27 February 1768, 29 May 1768, 19 November 1768, 27 May 1769, MGA F IV:77.

78 T. Lambrecht, 'Reciprocal Exchange, Credit and Cash: Agricultural Labour Markets and Local Economies in the Southern Low Countries during the Eighteenth Century', in *Continuity and Change*, vol 18, no 2 (2003); D.W. Sabean, *Property, Production, and Family in Neckarhausen 1700–1870* (Cambridge 1990).

79 Fontaine, *The moral Economy*; S. Hindle, *On the Parish? The Micro-Politics of Poor Relief in Rural England, c.1550–1750* (Oxford 2004), p. 76.

80 Lambrecht, 'Reciprocal Exchange', pp. 248–9.

81 Jacob, *The Clerical Profession*, p. 226.

82 Scott Dixon, *Reformation and Rural Society*, p. 83.

83 Malmstedt, *Bondetro och kyrkoro*, pp. 108–18

84 H. Levin, 'Bidrag till Visby stifts historia I', p. 191.

85 Polanyi, *The Great Transformation*, p. 48.

86 C. Ginzburg, 'Microhistory: Two or Three Things That I Know about It', in *Critical Inquiry*, vol 20, no 1 (1993), p. 21.

# A RECTOR IN WANT OF A WIFE

Beverly Tjerngren, Uppsala University

Most readers will recognize the first line of Jane Austen's *Pride and Prejudice*, written in the late eighteenth century and first published in 1813: 'It is a truth universally acknowledged, that a single man in possession of a good fortune, must be in want of a wife'. Thanks to Austen, as well as to significant historical research on the topic in recent decades, we are well aware of the central importance – socially, economically, and personally – of marriage in the early modern period. For the clergyman, marriage was also especially connected to religious and professional obligations. Without discounting the importance that these factors could also carry for non-clergy, it can be argued that their weight was greater – or at least great in a different way – for men of the cloth.

The Protestant reformers' disavowal of clerical celibacy went much farther than merely *allowing* priests to marry. Rather, they were *expected* to marry, to be 'the husband of one wife', as Luther's Small Catechism would have it.[1] Lyndal Roper has observed that marriage was the very heart of Reformation social order, within which the 'natural, complementary hierarchy of masculinity and femininity' was inscribed.[2]

In this paper I will delve down to the micro level in order to examine specifically the importance of marriage in creating a home for an early modern parish rector in rural Sweden, Adolph Adde. I will give an overview of his life and career and the role in these of marriage in general, and *his* marriage in particular. Key in this discussion will be a closer look at Adde's years as a widower, and what the evidence that remains from those years can reveal about what the loss of his wife might have meant to his home life.

Adolph Adde was born in 1704, a son of the mayor of Enköping,[3] an agrarian market town that, though past its heyday of the sixteenth and seventeenth centuries, remained an important local center for trade and agricultural production. Apart from the fact that he came from a socially and economically well placed family, little is known about Adde's upbringing. He began studying at Uppsala University at the age of

https://doi.org/10.16922/jrhlc.6.2.5

sixteen, was ordained at the age of twenty-nine, and after nearly twenty years spent in various lower clergy roles in the area, he was appointed rector in Kalmar parish in 1750. Adde served twelve years in this position before transferring to the post of rector in Lillkyrka parish in 1762, where he remained in service until his death in 1787.[4]

In the summer of 1751, less than a year after he assumed the office of rector in Kalmar, Adde married Margareta Hedvig Hultman. At the time of the marriage, the bride was nearly forty-eight years old and twice widowed. Her first marriage, at the age of twenty-one to a civil servant from Stockholm, resulted in the birth of one child, a daughter. After twenty-two years of marriage, Margareta was widowed for the first time, and not long afterward married Anders Welstadius, the rector in Kalmar parish.[5] She was Welstadius's third wife, and with the marriage she became stepmother to his eleven daughters and three sons, though the couple had no children together. The date of this marriage is uncertain, but the time between the death of Margareta's first husband and Welstadius's death in 1749 was only three years, meaning that this second marriage was relatively brief in duration.[6] Following Welstadius's death, it appears that Margareta did not maintain a relationship with her stepchildren, something that is not particularly surprising given that Welstadius's first two wives – the mothers of these children – were of high social and economic standing. The first was the illegitimate daughter of King Karl XI, and the second was the daughter of an academic and the close relative of a number of men who either had been or would ultimately be ennobled. The fourteen children of these two unions were well served in their own marriages and careers by these connections and surely had no need of a stepmother who had been married ever so briefly to their father.

Close readers may already have noticed a detail that it took me some time to see myself, and that is that Adolph Adde succeeded his wife's previous husband as rector of Kalmar parish. This means that the new couple was an example of a common practice in the early modern Swedish church known as 'widow conservation', in which the widow of a parish rector, or sometimes her eligible daughter, was married to her husband's successor to ensure her economic support.[7] While it is not unusual that Adde did not marry for the first time until he was in his forties and had been appointed rector, it is noteworthy that his bride was well past her child-bearing prime – at the time of the marriage she was approaching fifty years old. What's more, though she had been married for most of her adult life, Margareta had borne only one child, probably at least twenty years previously. It stands to reason, then, that Adde was not expecting his marriage to produce children. Adding weight to this argument is the fact that Margareta's daughter was unmarried and of eligible marriage age and, other possible considerations aside, it would have made more sense for Adde to conserve the rectory by marrying the daughter and continuing to provide for the mother.

All of these facts taken together suggest the possibility that what Adde was in want and need of, both personally and for the rectory, was a wife and a homemaker who would suit his life at the moment, not a young bride who would hopefully produce heirs and a legacy, and not a well placed spouse who brought with her valuable social connections. Unfortunately, there is nothing in the preserved record either to confirm or deny this interpretation. However, the evidence that does remain offers some revealing clues about the Adde marriage and the life and work they shared.

The church in Lillkyrka is a stone church that was built in medieval times and remains much the same in appearance as it did during Adde's time as rector there.[8] Unfortunately, the early modern rectory, built in 1729, no longer exists, but it was described in 1895 as being 'narrow, damp, and dark' consisting of a great room, two low chambers, a kitchen, and an attic loft.[9]

To judge from the available evidence, Adde enjoyed a successful career as parish rector. As we've seen, he transferred to Lillkyrka parish from Kalmar parish after twelve years, and during his time in Lillkyrka he was promoted to Dean in his own congregation in 1771, Vice Contract Dean in 1772, and ultimately Contract Dean in 1773.[10] Church historian Lars Otto Berg has noted that it is seldom seen that a clergyman is evaluated by his congregation as unanimously positively as Adde was. In his time he was appreciated as 'an unusually enterprising, diligent and knowledgeable man, judicious and with a keen interest in his work'.[11] In his obituary for Adde, curate Anders Adolph Borg described the rector as having 'an exceptionally happy nature', and being in possession of such godly patience and good temperament that even in a weak and elderly state he was, unlike others in a similar condition, 'seldom uncompassionate, acrimonious, suspicious, unkind, or irritable'. Rather, he met his pain and discomfort:

> with cheerfulness, being happy and satisfied, both on his own and among company of others; he was neither a burden to himself nor

> to others, and he was always welcome in the home of both the upper and the lower sorts, revered, admired, and beloved.[12]

Indeed, the rector was held in such high esteem by his congregants that it was often said around the village that his piety allowed him to hear not only the church bells, but also the very bells of Heaven.[13]

We see firsthand evidence of Adde's good nature in the obituary he wrote for his wife of twenty-seven years, following her death in 1778. He recounts that on her last day she was

> admirably lively, happy, cheerful, eating well and smiling for eight hours, albeit a little frenzied. But after dinner the labor of death began, though she listened to and understood words spoken and read wishing her a glorious departure. At six o'clock in the evening she bid me a joyous farewell and died without any straining or gasping.[14]

To be sure, the above passage speaks more explicitly to his late wife's demeanour than to his, but no small part of the rector's own character is revealed in his attentiveness to her to the very end.

We have all heard the aphorism 'happy wife, happy life', and its application to the Adde household seems apt. It is possible, of course, that all of this positivity is entirely down to Adolph Adde's own affability, and I am not in possession of any descriptions of the couple or their marriage that would either confirm or deny their happiness together. So, to further support my contention that Adde was a man who very much wanted – and needed – not just any wife, but his wife in particular, I turn now to those records I do have: the probate inventories drawn up after their respective deaths, hers in 1778 and his in 1787.

Early modern probate inventories are a source material that is abundantly available in Sweden, owing largely to a 1734 law that required they be recorded for all adults, female as well as male, unmarried as well as married.[15] That said, there do exist considerable gaps in the preservation of these inventories, and it is fairly unusual to have the records for both spouses in a marriage, especially outside the highest social classes. Not only are both Adolph Adde and Margareta Hedvig Hultman's inventories accessible, but the inventory drawn up for the estate of Anders Welstadius, Margareta's second husband, is also preserved. While Welstadius himself is only peripherally connected to this study, his probate inventory has helped me to sort out family relationships and to determine which, if any, objects in the Adde rectory might have originated in the Welstadius rectory.

The Welstadius household was relatively rich in land, goods, and money, but Margareta benefited little, if at all, from its wealth. It is noted throughout the inventory which children are to inherit which properties and/or possessions, but Margareta is not mentioned at all, apart from being named as Welstadius's widow. Her signature as witness at the end of the document is followed by the signatures of a number of Welstadius's in-laws from his earlier marriages, acting both as witnesses and guardians of minor children. At that point Margareta seems to have disappeared from Welstadius's circle entirely, taking with her only her right to continue living at the rectory (first through a so-called 'mercy year',[16] then through her marriage to her husband's successor). A comparison of Welstadius's probate inventory with Margareta's own shows no obvious overlap in possessions, indicating that his children did indeed inherit everything.[17]

Margareta Hedvig Hultman's probate inventory is nineteen pages long, well within what might have been seen as the 'normal' length of such documents for a woman of her standing. At the time of her death, the household – and it should be noted that the inventory covers the entire household at the time it was recorded, and not merely those possessions that could be considered 'hers' – was fairly well off, with the total value of the estate assessed to be 499 *riksdaler banco* (rdr). Debts and outstanding expenses of 175 rdr, or thirty-five per cent of the estate's value, are listed, leaving a net value of 324 rdr. This is not a vast fortune, to be sure, but it is an entirely respectable sum, especially considering that clergy families did not own the land on which they lived, and no immovable property is listed in the inventory.[18]

What is listed provides abundant evidence of a well appointed and comfortable home – narrowness, dampness, and darkness notwithstanding. Silver items, mostly of the sort intended for serving tea and formal meals, make up nearly twenty per cent of the estate's total value. Most of the household's finer kitchenware, including both coffee pots and teapots of higher value, was made of pewter. We also find a significant amount of copper cookware, including a coffee pot and two teapots – one larger, one smaller. Additionally, a porcelain tea service, with six teacups plus milk and sugar bowls, is listed along with a number of miscellaneous porcelain items. The listing for glass includes two sets of drinking glasses

– one a set of fourteen glasses, and the other a set of six – as well as a number of bottles and carafes.[19]

Bedclothes and household linens make up another large part of the inventory, accounting for approximately fifteen per cent of the estate's assessed worth. Considerable numbers of finer blankets and bedlinens are listed, along with good quality napkins, tablecloths, and towels, as well as four pairs of curtains. Further, at least five rooms (or parts of rooms) were adorned with wallpaper, and two large mirrors and a pair of wall clocks would surely have provided an added touch of refinement.[20]

All of these items were complemented by larger numbers of housewares and household textiles of more 'common' quality, and all of these trappings of housekeeping had to be stored and/or displayed somewhere. The inventory lists three oak cupboards, two small as well as one large and expensive, that were surely put to good use for both storage and display. Two food cupboards of a more utilitarian sort could be found in the kitchen, and several smaller, more decorative cupboards may well have held items their owners wanted to show off to their best advantage.[21]

Hospitality in the clergy household is a central theme of this issue, and a great many of the furnishings listed in Margareta Hedvig Hultman's probate inventory attest to its importance in the Adde rectory. Though the house itself was modest in size, it contained an abundance of seating furniture. The inventory lists two green-painted sofas, one of them smaller, and no fewer than thirty-five chairs of various types! In addition to nine ordinary wooden chairs, while Margareta was alive the rectory boasted the seating capacity of one dozen Russian-leather chairs, six upholstered Russian-leather chairs, six 'old' Russian-leather chairs with leather upholstery, one armchair with red cloth upholstery, two upholstered armchairs, and two older leather chairs.[22] Gudrun Andersson has identified Russian-leather chairs as following after armchairs in 'the hierarchy of chairs' in early modern elite Swedish homes, writing further that at least one set of a complete dozen chairs occupied a given place in elite furnishings.[23] The Adde rectory was well appointed, then, with respect to both domestic comfort and status manifestation.

The couple were no less well equipped where tables were concerned. Margareta's inventory lists two tea tables, two drop-leaf tables, and four 'small' tables of different sorts, in addition to a large, oblong table with a base, a round table with a base and drawers, and 'four tables to put together'.[24] With this relatively large and varied collection, together with the seating furniture listed above, the rector and his wife were prepared to receive guests in numbers great and small and to provide hospitality appropriate to visitors of all stations.

In addition to all of above goods and furnishings, the inventory lists a separate category with the heading 'Out in the Dean's building' (which I suspect is the 'Garden Office' that we will see later in Adde's own inventory). This category listing is nearly three pages long which – when we consider that livestock and farm products and equipment are also included in the inventory's total nineteen pages – makes clear that a significant portion of the household's domestic goods were kept in this space.[25] The presence of a writing desk and valuable collection of books (unfortunately not itemised in the inventory)[26] indicate the likelihood that Adde used this space for carrying out administrative work and probably also for meeting with parishioners. Many of the other contents indicate that this building or office was also a domestic space where sociable activity was carried out. As well the desk and the books, it held five small green-painted tables – one without drawers, one with drawers, and one with shelves, curtains, and drawers – a grey-painted table with ten drawers, a green-upholstered swivel chair, and a stuffed sofa. The space was also adorned with two mirrors, one large and one small, and many larger and smaller paintings and wall hangings, most with glass and gilded frames. Further, it contained a half-dozen wine glasses, four beer glasses, four chalices of various sizes, all with lids, a porcelain tea container with a stopper, a porcelain sugar bowls, four porcelain containers without description, and a container made of serpentine.[27]

The above paragraph does not give an exhaustive listing of all the items that were kept in the space specifically designated as Adde's own, but it is sufficient to demonstrate that he was a man who was accustomed to comfortable, elaborately appointed surroundings. In considering the entirety of the inventory, the abundance of home furnishings and housewares, as well as finer details such as small decorative boxes, paintings or other artwork in expensive frames, and the tools of hospitality, such as tea services and sets of glass drinking vessels, are testament that Adde and his wife, Margareta, had made a home and rectory that was well and truly lived-in.

This picture contrasts sharply with the one we see in the inventory drawn up after Adde's own death just nine years later. The dean and rector's inventory is only six pages long, including a full-page introduction that bequeaths all assets to two curates, one a nephew and the other whose relationship to Adde is unknown. The net value of the estate, after clearing debts and obligations adding up to seventy-six per cent of the total value, is only 36 rdr, approximately one-tenth the value of the households goods at the time of his wife's death.[28]

More striking still is the near disappearance of the niceties of home life and the trappings of hospitality that had characterized the rectory just nine years earlier. The house had been all but stripped of everything that went above what was strictly necessary for an elderly widower on his own. It is difficult not to notice that there is only one bed with accompanying bedding, one armchair, one larger table, and so forth. There are a few books, a couple of tobacco pipes and associated paraphernalia, some smaller portraits of the king and Martin Luther, and a few personal items such as shaving tools and clothing brushes, but very little in the way of extras. The bulk of the inventory is what we might call 'bits and bobs': small boxes containing 'assorted things', stray pieces of cloth too small to be useful, old and/or broken items long past their usefulness. More than a third of the total value of the estate, 58 rdr out of the total value of 155 rdr, is 'cash in several types of coin', presented in such a way to suggest that Adde had collected the money sort of willy-nilly, rather than consciously saving or putting it away.[29]

Especially poignant is the section of Adde's inventory under the heading 'In the Garden Office'. It takes up only a fraction of one page and has only thirteen listings, mostly miscellaneous flasks, bottles, and drinking vessels, but also two small tables and a number of 'old' wall hangings in the anteroom.[30] This meagre collection suggests that the space had been converted to a sort of storage area after Margareta's death.

Taken together, these inventories strongly reinforce the idea that a wife was necessary for the early modern clergyman, not only for the religious obligations set out by Martin Luther, but also for the creation of a home, in both the public sense that a rectory was the congregation's home, but also in the 'private' sense of small, homely comforts that exist between husband and wife.

To sum up, then, at the time of his wife's death, Adde's household was relatively well-off, owning all of the standard items one would expect to see in a respectable clergy household. The lists in his wife's probate inventory are replete with the trappings of homemaking and hospitality. When Adde himself died nine years later, the number of his possessions had diminished dramatically, to the point that he was nearly without assets. Not only that, but the later inventory shows a marked lack of the aforementioned items relating to homemaking and hospitality, revealing instead a man who had pared his material life down to the bare necessities. Without his wife, Adde appears to have lost all interest not only in keeping up appearances, but also in keeping a home.

I'm moved to conclude the way that I started, with a quotation from *Pride and Prejudice*, a few fitting lines from the otherwise insufferable Mr. Collins that I'm certain Adolph Adde would have appreciated:

> 'My reasons for marrying are, first, that I think it a right thing for every clergyman in easy circumstances (like myself) to set the example of matrimony in his parish; secondly, that I am convinced that it will add very greatly to my happiness.'

## Notes

1 K. Stadin, *Stånd och genus i stormaktstidens Sverige* (Lund, 2004), p. 170.

2 L. Roper, *The Holy Household: Women and Morals in Reformation Augsburg* (Oxford, 1989), p. 164.

3 Uppsala Landsarkiv (hereafter ULA), Parish Records, Enköping C:2 Birth and Baptism Book, entry from 17–18 October 1704, p. 225.

4 L.O. Berg, et al., *Uppsala stifts herdaminne II.8:1 Trögds kontrakt* (Uppsala, 2004), pp. 157–8.

5 ULA, Parish Records, Lillkyrka F:1 Death and Burial Book, entry from 17 February 1778, pp. 154–5. L.O. Berg, et al., *Uppsala stifts herdaminne II.8:1 Trögds kontrakt* (Uppsala, 2004), pp. 157. Berg gives her name as "Hedvig Margareta Hultman", but the consulted primary sources record her name as "Margareta Hedvig".

6 ULA, Håbo District Court Archive, probate inventory of Welstadius's estate 12 May 1750, FI:1, nr. 71.

7 G. Malmstedt, *Bondetro och kyrkoro: Religiös mentalitet i stormaktstidens Sverige* (Lund, 2002), pp. 82–3.

8 L.O. Berg, et al., *Uppsala stifts herdaminne II.8:1 Trögds kontrakt* (Uppsala, 2004), p. 131.

9 *Ibid.*, p. 130.

10 *Ibid.*, p. 158.

11 *Ibid.*, pp. 158–9.

12 ULA, Parish Records, Lillkyrka F:1 Death and Burial Book, entry from 11 April 1787, pp. 177–8.

13 L.O. Berg, et al., *Uppsala stifts herdaminne II.8:1 Trögds kontrakt* (Uppsala, 2004), pp. 159–60.

14 ULA, Parish Records, Lillkyrka F:1 Death and Burial Book, entry from 17 February 1778, pp. 154–5.

15 G. Andersson, *Stadens dignitärer: Den lokala elitens status- and maktmanifestation i Arboga 1650–1770* (Stockholm, 2009), p. 133.

16 R. Norrman, *Konserverade änkor och kvinnor på undantag: Prästänkornas villkor i Uppsala stift 1720–1920 – från änkehjälp till familjepension* (Uppsala, 1993), p. 37.

17 ULA, Håbo District Court Archive, probate inventory of Welstadius's estate 12 May 1750, FI:1, nr. 71.

18 ULA, Trögds District Court Archive, probate inventory of Hultman's estate 26 March 1778, F:4a, nr. 285.

19 *Ibid.*

20 *Ibid.*

21 *Ibid.*

22 *Ibid.*

23 Andersson 2009, pp. 156–7.

24 ULA, Trögds District Court Archive, probate inventory of Hultman's estate 26 March 1778, F:4a, nr. 285.

25 *Ibid.*

26 *Ibid.*

27 *Ibid.*

28 ULA, Trögds District Court Archive, probate inventory of Adde's estate 2 May 1787, F:6, nr. 171.

29 *Ibid.*

30 *Ibid.*

# GENTEEL OR RESPECTABLE? THE MATERIAL CULTURE OF RURAL CLERGY IN LATE GEORGIAN ENGLAND

Jon Stobart, Manchester Metropolitan University

In August 1790, the Northampton auctioneer Mr Rouse published 'A catalogue of the entire elegant, genteel and useful household furniture, plate, linen, china, books, and other valuable effect of the Revd Zacharias Rose, A.M., late Rector of Broughton and Draughton'.[1] As this announcement makes very clear, the houses of the rural clergy could contain a wide variety of high quality furnishings. It underlines that men such as the Revd Rose often formed part of the elite in English villages, elevated in economic and material as well as social terms. They occupied what was frequently the largest house in the village and sometimes enjoyed close links with the local gentry. These connections reflected the rise in social standing of certain sections of the clergy through the eighteenth century and were reinforced by the common practice of using lucrative livings as a means of setting up the younger sons or cadet branches of landed gentry families.[2] As William Bray noted of the Drake family of Amersham: 'one of the gentleman's sons is presented by him to the living, which, from its value, and the goodness and situation of the parsonage house, is no bad establishment for a younger son'.[3] Such sinecures, and the pluralism which characterised the eighteenth and early nineteenth centuries, meant that parsons were often well-connected and well-housed. Bax has described in detail the ways in which prosperous clergymen were willing and able to rebuild their houses, a practice which Parson Woodforde noted in one of his neighbours, the Revd Mr Attle. After visiting his neighbour in April 1779, Woodforde recorded that he had 'a noble house and his fields about him look exceeding neat and well. He built the House himself and it cost him 1000 Pound'.[4] He also noted that he had taken coffee and tea with Attle, but he made no comment on the interior of the house or its decoration and furnishings.

https://doi.org/10.16922/jrhlc.6.2.6

Like Woodforde, historians have shown relatively little interest in the material lives of the clergy, beyond broad attacks on eighteenth-century venality, from which they are slowly being rescued.[5] Where this has been attempted, attention has been focused firmly on the architecture of the parsonage or on the episcopate rather than on ordinary clergymen.[6] In Lorna Weatherill's analysis of changing domestic material culture in late seventeenth- and early eighteenth-century England, the clergy are placed with 'trades of high status'.[7] They are thus one notch down from the gentry, but they shared similar patterns of ownership in the key goods on which her analysis was focused. Weatherill's primary purpose was to trace change in English homes, rather than to determine what said change might tell us about social standing. However, the shifting patterns of ownership that she identified were part of longer term changes that were apparent much earlier. Indeed, the widening attraction and accessibility of luxury consumption was already a social phenomenon in the sixteenth century when William Harrison noted that it had spread 'even unto the inferior artificers and many farmers' who had 'learned also to garnish their cupboards with plate, their joint beds with tapestry and silk hangings, and their tables with carpets and fine napery'.[8] For Harrison and for many other commentators, this was an alarming trend, one that threatened to break down a long established system of material markers that distinguished different social groups. Rising incomes amongst the middling sort created increasingly blurred distinctions of wealth and opened up new possibilities for consumption, fuelled in part by the influx of new goods and commodities.[9] Elsewhere in Europe, this led to the imposition and reiteration of sumptuary laws; in England, such legislation was much less common and largely unenforced, even when enacted.[10] There was a social and material fluidity that could be exploited by individuals and social groups to realign themselves within the social hierarchy. This was most apparent in terms of personal appearance, leading to confusion and sometimes despair about who was a gentleman and how they might be identified. As Guy Miege noted as early as 1699 that anyone with 'either a liberal or genteel education, that looks gentleman-like (whether he be so or not) and has the wherewithal to live freely and handsomely, is by the courtesy of England usually called a gentleman'.[11] However, this blurring of boundaries was also apparent in the domestic setting – as Harrison makes clear. People could render themselves genteel through their drawing rooms as well as their dress. Alongside country seats and villas for the gentry, architectural treatises offered models for elegant parsonages and farmhouses for the socially ambitious who could also draw on furniture pattern books to commission tasteful pieces from local craftsmen.[12]

In this paper, I draw on a sample of twenty-one sale catalogues for rural clergymen in Northamptonshire, in the English Midlands, between 1761 and 1842 to discover the nature and quality of their domestic material culture. The sample is modest and it is clear that sales did not always involve all the goods in the house, but auction catalogues provide a unique insight into domestic material culture in the late eighteenth and early nineteenth centuries, not least because they provide much richer descriptions of household goods than we see in inventories, in part because of the imperative to sell. My concern is twofold. First, I want to examine their ownership of a range of luxury and semi-luxury goods, broadly defined, as it is revealed through the goods being sold, generally post-mortem. In particular, I am concerned with the extent to which their belongings compare with those of the gentry of the county and allowed these clergymen to align themselves with genteel and tasteful domestic life. Building on this, I then explore the ways in which their possessions were described in the sale catalogues, using this as a mechanism for assessing the quality of goods but also as an indication of the broader systems of taste and cultural norms with which the clergy might be aligned. Ultimately, my aim is to determine whether these material possessions positioned their clergy owners as genteel or merely respectable, or whether they suggest a more specific social niche that was particular to the prosperous clergy.

## Household goods: markers of status

Rather than examine the full range of goods to be found in clergymen's houses, I want to focus here on those items that marked their status. This is not because the pots and pans in the kitchen or the pillows and blankets in the bedrooms were unimportant; far from it, they tell us much about daily life in even the grandest of houses.[13] However, other types of goods were more obviously important and conspicuous in carrying messages about the wealth and status of the owner, and in marking them out from other sections of society. For Thorstein Veblen, consumption by the leisure classes

> undergoes a specialisation as regards the quality of the goods consumed. Since the consumption of these more excellent goods is an evidence of wealth, it becomes honorific; and conversely the failure to consume in due quantity and quality becomes a mark of inferiority and demerit.[14]

Defining the precise character of these 'excellent goods' is problematic.[15] Thinking of them purely in terms of luxury is unhelpful; rather, they were positional goods in that their value was used to mark out status, but their excellence was not merely a reflection of cost, but also encompassed notions of discernment, as Veblen put it, 'to discriminate with some nicety between the noble and the ignoble in consumable goods'.[16] Looking back from the early twentieth century, Sombart drew on contemporary sources to argue that domestic luxury formed the area of enormous and growing expenditure: crystal lamps, busts and medallions, carved marble chimneys, Asian textiles, gilded furniture and magnificent clocks.[17] The impression is confirmed by Amanda Vickery's analysis of the Georgian interior, although she notes that new forms of luxury goods were balanced by others that were more established, much of the spending of mid-eighteenth-century gentlemen still being centred on coaches, horses and wine cellars.[18] I have argued elsewhere that the houses of the lesser gentry were characterised by a widening array of such goods and that many of them were sold off in house sales when they died.[19] My question here is whether the clergy were part of this same material culture.

Enumerating the types of goods listed in the sale catalogues reveals that these two groups had much in common (Table 1). Unsurprisingly, furniture, mirrors and curtains, and glass and chinaware were found in the vast majority of sales, the exceptions coming when the auction focused on libraries (as at the rectory in Stilton in 1807) or where auctions appear to have been selling off specific items, sometimes following earlier sales at the same house (Geddington in 1828 and 1829). Prints, paintings, clocks and linens were found in forty to fifty per cent of both gentry and clergy sales, the modest showing of the last of these reflecting a general decline in the sale at house auctions at least of second-hand textiles, despite the continued importance of linen to displays of polite dining and cleanliness.[20] Much the same was true of ornamental items, musical instruments and scientific equipment, where ownership amongst the clergy was only slightly lower than amongst

Table 1. Presence of categories of goods in catalogues for gentry and clergy house sales in Northamptonshire, 1761–1842

| | Gentry (n=24) | | Clergy (n=21) | |
|---|---|---|---|---|
| | Number | Percentage | Number | Percentage |
| Furniture, mirrors & curtains | 24 | 100 | 20 | 95 |
| Glass & chinaware | 20 | 83 | 20 | 95 |
| Table and household linen | 11 | 46 | 8 | 38 |
| Prints & paintings | 17 | 71 | 13 | 62 |
| Books | 8 | 33 | 13 | 62 |
| Scientific instruments | 11 | 46 | 6 | 29 |
| Wine | 9 | 38 | 4 | 19 |
| Silverware | 10 | 42 | 3 | 14 |
| Carriages | 7 | 35 | 8 | 38 |
| Collections & antiques | 8 | 33 | 0 | 0 |

Source: Volumes of auction catalogues, Northamptonshire Central library, M0005644-7NL

the gentry. More surprising, perhaps, is that carriages appeared in the sale catalogues of clergymen as often as they did those of gentlemen, an indication of the social standing of the former, but also their wealth: a carriage also meant keeping one or more horses, although it is more likely that the clergymen were using the same horses for riding.[21]

The key areas where the clergy and gentry diverged in their material culture – at least in considering the types of things found in their homes – came in terms of books, wine, silverware and collections, including antiques. These can all be viewed as positional goods, but their different importance in gentry and clergy houses points to a slight divergence in the construction and articulation of their social standing. Sales from the houses of clergymen were twice as likely to include books, although – as with country house libraries – the size and composition of these clergy libraries varied considerably.[22] The books of the Revd Haggit in Rushton were auctioned off in 1798 in just twenty-nine lots, but in many other cases there were dozens or even hundreds of lots, many containing a number of books or books that came in several volumes; the largest was the 511 lots required to clear the library of the Revd Speidell at Crick in 1836.[23] Naturally the core of these libraries comprised books on religion – bibles, sermons, lexicons, and the like – but many were far more wide-ranging. The Revd Speidell owned books on religion, but also volumes of poems, plays and music, histories, guides, dictionaries, medical books and novels; the Revd Laurence in East Farndon (where the sale took place in 1838) had books on history, government and gardening, plus several journals.[24] In this, clergy libraries were similar in composition and sometimes size to many country house libraries and no doubt carried similar messages of learning and status – something which is perhaps unsurprising given the shared university education of sections of the gentry and clergy.[25] It is also clear that at least some clergymen were discerning bibliophiles, their libraries containing numerous books from the seventeenth and even the sixteenth centuries, sometimes held in high quality bindings. At Crick, there were seventeenth-century histories and bibles; a copy of Lodge's *Portraits of Illustrious Personages of Great Britain* (1821) described as 'a choice copy, fine impressions, calf elegant, gilt leaves'; and Clarendon's *History of the Rebellion* (1816), which is listed as 'uncut' – an indication that the clergy sometimes owned books for display as well as reading.[26] At Ecton in 1838, the Revd Whalley had a Latin Testament from 1582, Luther's *Commentary* from 1588 and a 1601 edition of Ovid in Latin – just a handful of a much bigger collection of old books.[27] Like those in the country houses of gentlemen, these clergy libraries were to be read and studied, but also displayed and admired. That they often took as many days to auction off as the rest of the household goods speaks of the interest they held for buyers, no doubt including other clergy and gentlemen.

Beyond the library, what these clergy house sales lacked in comparison with their gentry counterparts were some of the established markers of status, what de Vries describes as old luxury: goods distinguished by their exclusiveness, cost and complexity.[28] This might be seen in terms of individual items: elaborate cabinets such as that sold from Rolleston Hall in 1801 which was described in the catalogue as a 'mahogany case of four large, and two small compress drawers; the upper part, with folding doors, encloses a valuable ebony cabinet, *the fronts of the drawers of which are* MOST DELICATELY PENCILLED *with the history of the journeying the Israelites in the Wilderness, and a great number of exquisite miniature figures*'.[29] Old luxury might also be seen in an impressive array of silverware or in collections of coins, medallions or rare china. These are seen in the houses of the gentry, for example, the 'plaster bustos' and 'Five Collections of Medals in plaster, fram'd and glaz'd' sold at Cottingham in 1762 or the coin collection belonging to J.P. Clarke, esquire (1830), which ran to sixteen lots including: English and foreign silver coins, provincial coins, and Greek and Roman coins (the latter carefully categorised by Caesar), and silver medals.[30] Such items were not wholly absent from the homes of clergymen – there were marble slab tables at Broughton and Crick, whilst the Revd Goode at Weldon (1761) had 'Seven pieces of curious Tapestry, containing the History of Moses'.[31] However, when they do appear, they are often one-off items or the quantities are relatively modest. The Revd Speidell at Crick was exceptional in owning four hundred ounces of silver; more typical were his counterparts at Broughton (1790) and Orlingbury (1824), where there were just seventeen and sixteen pieces of silver being sold in total.[32] Nor were these pieces engraved with arms and crests like those owned by titled aristocrats. In this, they had much in common with their gentry neighbours whose silverware was similarly unadorned.

Similar qualitative differences were apparent in their prints and paintings, and their scientific instruments. The latter appears in the homes of several clergymen including the Revd Reynolds at Little Bowden (1830), who was clearly interested in astronomy, yet his investment does not appear to have run beyond a telescope and stand. His contemporary, the Revd Durham of Burton Latimer (1833), had a solar microscope and an electrifying machine, both of which speak of a practical interest in science, albeit one that was fairly limited in scope and in its material manifestation.[33] Such modest equipment parallels that seen in several gentry houses in the sample: the 1829 sale at Geddington, for example, included a 'handsome telescope', but no other scientific equipment, whilst the un-named owner of Wollaston Hall had a fairly impressive three telescopes, globe and pedometer. Yet even this pales in comparison with the extensive collections assembled by some wealthy landowners. Edward, Fifth Baron Leigh, spent £27 7s on an air pump, syringes, receivers, cylinder glasses, funnels, hemispheres, and other equipment from Edward Nairne, a noted scientific instrument maker of Cornhill in London.[34]

It is possible, then, to see these prosperous clergymen as materially and socially aligned with the lesser gentry. This is especially apparent in their possession of an array of objects which allowed them to engage in the kind of polite and increasingly informal sociability which marked gentility. In de Vries's analysis this was 'new luxury': socially inclusive and linked to refined practices and performances of taste and sociability.[35] This is best illustrated in the ownership of tasteful and comfortable furniture, the equipage for tea drinking and social dining, and the more general gathering together of such things in assemblages that marked rooms as spaces of refined sociability. Taking these in turn, many of the sale catalogues itemise an array of furniture, often en suite, which would create an informal and comfortable room. In his drawing room at Titchmarsh (1788), the Revd Pye had a mahogany-framed sofa covered with green morine; a set of twelve armed chairs, 'painted India bamboo pattern' with green morine seats; a Wilton carpet and green morine curtains. There were two mahogany card tables, a mahogany Pembroke table, and three small fire screens.[36] His family and guests could thus sit in comfort whilst playing cards, reading or talking – either together or in small groups. Similarly, the Revd Whalley at Ecton (1838) could accommodate his guests on a large sofa, a couch, an ottoman, four easy chairs and five chairs, each with chintz covers. The white-and-gold carved pier table, ormolu-mounted chiffonier, and pair of 'fancy' tables added a touch of grandeur to the room, but there was also a work table, writing table, loo table, book stand, a small bookcase, a Canterbury and what-not, and a set of occasional tables.[37] These were the kinds of pieces that DeJean calls 'convenience furniture' and would have made Whalley's drawing room both comfortable and convenient.[38]

Dining and tea drinking were rendered polite and genteel performances by the use of fashionable porcelain and silverware. The latter was rarely seen in the sales at clergy houses, but when it did appear silverware generally comprised cutlery, candlesticks, decanter stands and cruets, all of which would have added shine to the dining table. Porcelain was far more widely owned, generally being listed in terms of sets for dining, or for drinking tea, coffee and more occasionally chocolate. Fairly typical is the chinaware owned by the Revd Rose at Broughton. He had a dinner service comprising forty-two plates, eighteen dessert plates, twelve soup plates, and an assortment of serving plates and dishes, including a covered soup tureen and a salad bowl. He also had a set comprising tea pot, twelve tea cups and saucers, twelve coffee cups and saucers, a sugar bowl and a water bowl, plus two smaller tea sets, several sets of cups and saucers, and numerous individual pieces. Of particular note is that five of his teapots were black. Kate Smith has noted how these were especially prized in showing off the delicate white hands of the hostess who would be pouring the tea and elegance of her movements in undertaking these duties.[39] Their presence in the rectory at Broughton suggests that Pye and his wife were engaged in such genteel performances and were aware of the prevailing fashion in chinaware and polite entertaining. The rooms in which this porcelain would have been used were themselves embodiments of new luxury. The Revd Rose's Best Parlour contained a pair of dining tables, eight chairs, a cellaret, a tea chest and a tea caddy, all made from mahogany; there was also a tea caddy and a backgammon table. On the walls hung a series of prints, including a mezzotint of David Garrick in the character of Macbeth, two landscapes and a copy of a Van Dyke painting. Next-door, in the Little Parlour, there were four chairs, a window seat and a pair of 'slope-sided easy chairs', together with a Pembroke table and two card tables. Together they formed almost copybook examples of the kind of domestic environment created for refined and polite entertaining.[40]

## Describing goods, declaring quality and defining culture

The clergymen examined here had houses that spoke of more than respectability; the range of high status goods indicates alignment with ideals of gentility and, more specifically, with the material culture of their gentry neighbours. Yet many of these goods were also found in the homes of the urban middling sort. They too owned mahogany furniture, chintz curtains and Staffordshire porcelain, as well as books, silverware, clocks and the like. In this sense, there was often no hard divide between different sections of society in terms of the *types* of things that were found in their homes. The landowning classes might distinguish themselves through the size of their houses and their possession of old luxuries, which remained beyond the reach of most householders by virtue of their cost, the 'reach' needed to acquire them, and their semiotic complexity.[41] More generally, however, distinctions might be made in terms of the *quality* of particular items. There was kudos in owning damask tablecloths, rosewood furniture, Dresden porcelain and copies of paintings by old masters. Quality can be elusive in inventories, but it is often apparent in the descriptions of goods in auction catalogues. Here, I examine three aspects of this: descriptions of the physical characteristics of individual pieces, indications of the provenance of objects, and the use of adjectives to describe the material or aesthetic qualities of a wide range of household goods. Together, these can offer invaluable insights into the domestic material culture of the clergy: the ways in which their possessions were framed by linguistic and cultural contexts.[42]

Auction catalogues reflect an imperative to sell, which no doubt encouraged auctioneers to talk up the quality and thus the value of the objects available. Some auctioneers reacted by eschewing florid descriptions; the sale catalogues for the rectories at Titchmarsh and Cranford St Andrew (1822), for example, included materials and sizes, but there is no attempt to enthuse the potential buyer through eloquent pen portraits of the goods on offer.[43] Thus we see in the dining parlour at Titchmarsh a 'mahogany dining-table, 3 feet 8 inches', a 'chimney glass, painted frame, middle plate 27 by 15, end plates 15 by 14', and a 'pair of blue spun silk festoon window-curtains'.[44] Taking this a stage further, the auctioneer organising the 1787 sale at Islip Mills, declared in the catalogue that

> 'Bombast Puffing of Pictures, as well as of other Articles, is always ridiculous; as not furnishing any just or clear Ideas by which the unskilled may form any judgment of their Merits, but at the same time never fails to excite the Laughter and Contempt of the Connisseur [*sic*].[45]

Few followed this lead and auctioneers frequently offered lengthy and persuasive descriptions. The listing for the cabinet at Rolleston Hall, noted earlier, was particularly lengthy, but two or three lines were frequently accorded to items including curtains, sofas, dressing tables and mirrors, detailing their size, materials, colour and finish.[46]

Sale catalogues for parsonages rarely reached quite the same rhetorical heights, but many offered detailed and sometimes rather florid descriptions. This was especially true for the larger and more grandly furnished rectories where sales continued for several days. This was certainly true at Broughton (six days), Ecton (five days) and especially Crick (six days) where we see countless items described in ways that closely mirror the entries in gentry sale catalogues. In room seven at Crick, a bed chamber, we have a 'superior Spanish mahogany double wash-handstand, with rising top, dressing glass, 2 drawers, and kneehole, on turned legs and castors', and in the drawing room, we find 'two pair of elegant blue merino damask window curtains, trimmed with silk gymp, deep fringed valens, holders and tassels, carved imitative oak cornices, laths and rods'.[47] Even at small sales, such as that of the possessions of the Revd Henry Hoare in 1809, the auctioneer could wax lyrical, the best bed room containing a 'handsome mahogany fluted pillar'd lath bottom bedstead (5 feet 9 wide) white striped dimity furniture, elegant drapery, rich chints border, japan cornice, festoon window-curtain to correspond (*by Siddons*)'.[48] Not only do such descriptions suggest a more active attempt to sell the goods on the part of the auctioneer, they also provide a vivid image of the material qualities of these clergymen's belongings. These were well-furnished houses, on a par with their gentry neighbours in both the quantity and quality of their furnishings.

As is apparent from the description of the washstand at Crick, provenance was sometimes an important point of reference. It tells us something of the material qualities of the object and also indicates its economic or cultural value. Here again, we can see the clergy houses occupying a similar world to those of the gentry, but perhaps lacking the kudos afforded by the presence of metropolitan and European luxury goods. The catalogue for the 1823 sale at Geddington House, for instance, made much of the fact that the furniture was 'principally supplied by Messrs. GILLOWS, within these Three Years', and the lots included a variety of decorative French porcelain.[49] Nonetheless, the makers' names were included against a wide variety of items, no doubt to underline the quality and desirability of the items being sold. Most frequently named was Wedgwood porcelain, the cachet of the maker sometimes being underlined by the fashionability of the design, as at the rectory in Broughton where a 'Table-set of the neat much improved Staffordshire Ware with the greatly admired Blue-tinged Edges, which gives it all the genteel Effect of a Service of China'.[50] The phrasing here is revealing: in telling potential buyers that Staffordshire ware is 'much improved' and the particular design is 'greatly admired', the auctioneer was offering reassurance about the material and visual qualities of the porcelain as well as its symbolic value as tasteful tableware. The goods are thus simultaneously situated in commercial, aesthetic and cultural contexts that aligned them with gentility. Worcester and Dresden porcelain were also itemised at Crick and elsewhere, indicating that there was some discernment being shown about which manufacturer might produce the most desirable items for particular use. The makers were again identified for many of the musical and scientific instruments being offered for sale: a Collard piano at Crick, a flute by Clementi and a piano by Goulding, D'Alamain & Co. at Corby; a Borrowman piano and Newton globes at Cranford St Andrew.[51] To some extent, all of these might be seen as branded goods: a known and trusted name acting as a symbol and guarantor of the quality of the piece. As such, it links the clergy into a more modern world of brands and mass consumerism that might be viewed as being at odds with attempts to distinguish themselves through their material culture. In reality, and with the possible exception of the Staffordshire ware of Wedgwood and others, these were far from being goods aimed at a mass market. A piano from Borrowman of Soho, for example, said much about the reach and knowledge of the consumer because such items were not available locally in Northamptonshire – except, of course, from sales such as these.

Provenance could also be signalled in a more general sense, most frequently through identifying goods by their country of origin, although these should not always be taken at face value. For example, the Revd Pye at Titchmarsh owned a diverse range of porcelain, including a 'breakfast set of blue and white Nankeen', a 'fine large India punch-bowl', and a 'complete long set of burnt-in fine India tea-china'. Whether this was genuine Chinese porcelain is impossible to tell, but the label remains significant in that it signalled an association with the Orient that was tangible as much as cultural.[52] Much the same is true of the 'Five raised Figures of India Birds, in four Japan Frames, viz. Chinese Painted Cock Pheasant,– Long-tailed Parrket – Purple and white Chinese Cock and Hen Phesant – and Blue, Red and Yellow Maccaw' found in the closet adjoining the Best Chamber in the rectory at Broughton.[53] Both the character and likely provenance of the goods linked these rural rectories to a wider world of empire and commerce, but also of cultural cosmopolitanism and exoticism.[54] Such associations are most strikingly illustrated in a single object: the 'handsome tiger skin' found in the Revd Whalley's drawing room in Ecton. There is no way of knowing how this came to rural Northamptonshire, but even if it was acquired via a London dealer or from another house sale, it speaks of an imaginative connection to the Orient and an immersion in a growing taste for the exotic. This was seen throughout Whalley's house: the kingwood and rosewood furniture in his drawing room, the Turk's head on the stairs or the inlaid Indian chest and two 'beautifully carved ivory candlesticks' in a bedroom.[55] Like his landowning neighbours, Whalley was deeply immersed in the material culture of empire in terms of the provenance of materials and specific objects, and a more general aesthetic. Again like in many country houses, these things were spread throughout the rectory at Ecton, making it difficult to determine the precise meaning and impact of these objects.[56] The catalogues alone do not tell us if this clergyman was subscribing to the imperial project through his material culture or if he had a particular taste for the exotic, or if he was less self-aware and simply following the dictates of fashion.

As the descriptions of Whalley's tiger skin and ivory candlesticks indicate, the quality of items was also communicated through the use of adjectives. These tied goods into wider systems of aesthetics, taste and cultural norms, and were deployed both on the catalogue covers and alongside descriptions of individual items.[57] Unlike the sales of goods from gentry houses, auctioneers made no claim that the goods sold from clergy houses were 'genuine', presumably because it was felt that there was no need to assert their authenticity in this way. In this context, 'genuine' connects goods to the householder and acts as an indicator of social capital: the potential buyer is reassured about the quality of the goods on offer (they are not detritus from previous sales) and is simultaneously linked to the previous owner.[58] The latter would matter more if the goods being sold once belonged to the earl of Halifax or came from Kirby Hall; it became less important in the case of vicars and parsonages. The most common descriptions on the covers of catalogues for clergy sales fall into three groups. First, there were assertions that the things being offered for sale were 'valuable' and 'modern', together seen in nearly half of the catalogues. The former is a reminder that used goods retained economic value and that second-hand was by no means the resort of the poor. The latter indicates the cultural currency of the objects; if not exactly fashionable, they are at least up to date and would thus form suitable adornments in respectable or even genteel houses. Second was the claim that these things were 'useful', a quality that might most obviously link to kitchenware and husbandry ware (important elements of many sales, but beyond the scope of this paper), but also a reminder of Maxine Berg's argument that many items becoming available to householders through the eighteenth century were attractive because of their utility as well as their novelty.[59] It is significant, therefore, that useful was always deployed in conjunction with genteel: these goods would bring practical and symbolic benefits to their new owners. This takes us to the third set of labels, those which carried aesthetic and social meanings. For Vickery, genteel and elegant 'embodied the social distinctions of provincial gentility' and helped to tie these goods and the clergymen who had owned them to the sphere of their gentry neighbours.[60]

Inside the catalogues, the language changes. As with the gentry catalogues, usefulness and value disappear and the goods are described either in terms of their declared quality (excellent, capital) or aesthetic qualities (handsome, elegant, neat).[61] However, the use of descriptive language in catalogues for clergy sales is both less widespread and less diverse than in gentry catalogues (Table 2). Of the 14 catalogues that included some qualitative descriptions, five deployed 'excellent', mostly to describe furniture. This ranged from to the 'most excellent 8-day dial clock' sold from the rectory at Rushton to the 'excellent Spanish mahogany-framed dressing glass' at Ecton.[62] Its precise meaning is difficult to discern, but it certainly communicated the superior quality of the piece in terms of workmanship, design and materials. This becomes more apparent in a phrase used for several items in the sale at Corby (1842) where the dining room contained a 'very excellent town-made set of mahogany dining tables' and a 'very excellent town-made mahogany sideboard'. These contrasted with the following item – a 'mahogany cheffonier [*sic*] with drawers' – in a way that emphasises the superior quality of the first two items, where their excellence is layered onto their metropolitan provenance, the one reinforcing the other.[63] Much thus could be said of the superlative 'capital', which was also used in conjunction with town-made to underline the quality of the piece – effectively declaring it as the best quality.[64] This term was deployed for a wider range of goods, including firearms. There was a 'capital fowling piece, silver mounted' in the rectory at Braybrooke (1828) and another 'capital fowling piece, with roller lock and gold touch hole *by Steele*' at Lowick rectory (1816).[65] In both cases, the gun was identified as being of superior quality in terms of materials and manufacture. Applied to furniture, it appears to have signified particularly large or impressive pieces, such as the 'set of capital solid Spanish mahogany dining tables on extending frames and massive reeded legs, with brass castors, 5 ft wide and 14 ft 7 long' sold at Crick.[66]

From such descriptions, it is clear that a number of rectories contained impressive, well made and high quality furnishings. However, it was aesthetic descriptions that were most frequently deployed; indeed, all the catalogues that included qualitative descriptions used at least one of these terms (Table 2). Almost anything could be handsome, from the 'two pair of handsome brass candlesticks' at Grafton Underwood (1794), and the 'handsome chintz French window curtain, lined and fringed' at Rothwell (1816), to the 'set of handsome mahogany telescope dining tables, with circular ends' at East Farndon (1838).[67] As with capital, this indicated to late eighteenth-century lexicographers like James Barclay ideas of grandeur or dignity, and a sense of beauty and grace.[68] Two generations later, it was being layered with additional meanings, Charles Richardson defining it 'cleverly or skilfully done; and thus, further, suitable or well adapted' – a very fitting description for well made furniture.[69]

Table 2. Adjectival descriptors of goods listed in catalogues for gentry and clergy house sales in Northamptonshire, 1761–1842

| | Gentry (n=24) | | Clergy (n=21) | |
|---|---|---|---|---|
| | Number | Percentage | Number | Percentage |
| Fine | 14 | 58 | 1 | 5 |
| Excellent | 11 | 45 | 5 | 24 |
| Capital | 8 | 33 | 6 | 29 |
| Superior | 1 | 4 | 2 | 10 |
| Handsome | 16 | 67 | 11 | 52 |
| Elegant | 11 | 45 | 5 | 24 |
| Neat | 8 | 33 | 8 | 38 |
| Beautiful | 9 | 38 | 1 | 5 |
| Genteel | 2 | 8 | 0 | 0 |
| Curious | 3 | 13 | 0 | 0 |
| Valuable | 2 | 8 | 0 | 0 |

Source: Volumes of auction catalogues, Northamptonshire Central library, M0005644-7NL

At both gentry and clergy sales, 'elegant' was used to describe a variety of furniture, mirrors and chinaware. Contemporary definitions linked it specifically with gentility, refining the idea of status with that of beauty. As Barclay put it: '*genteel* implies something above the common run; elegant means beautiful without grandeur'. Remarkably, his definition focused specially on furniture: 'By a house *genteelly* furnished is understood a house containing every necessary, good and creditable; by *elegantly* furnished is meant *genteelly*, and in such a manner as to please without elevation'. Elegance was thus a refinement of taste and beauty, to which Richardson added notions of discernment and the sense of something 'highly wrought, highly polished'.[70] These complex meanings are well illustrated in the drawing room at Crick. The rosewood what-not, Canterbury and chess table were all 'handsome'; the rosewood Davenport writing desk was 'capital'; the case for the piano was 'superb', and the plate chimney glass was 'noble' and 'brilliant'. Alongside these were a 'very elegant 6-ft carved rosewood Grecian chaise longue', 'a very elegant 5-ft winged rosewood commode, with carved pilasters', 'a pair of elegant flower-pattern and gold china candlesticks', and 'a pair of very elegantly carved rosewood pole fire-screens'.[71] These pieces were elegant in the sense of beauty without grandeur, and in their workmanship and finish; both furniture and description linked the parsonage with gentility.

Notably absent from the list of adjectives used by the auctioneers at Crick was the word 'neat', although they deployed it elsewhere in the house. It carried connotations of elegance and skill, but 'void either of splendour or dignity' as Barclay put it. For Amanda Vickery, it conveyed restrained good taste and, as she observes, was often used to describe wallpapers.[72] As with gentry sales, its application in the clergy sale catalogues appears to connote similar meanings of modest good taste. At the rectory in Braybrooke, the drawing room contained a 'neat mahogany sofa' and a 'neat mahogany bookcase with glazed folding door & secretaire'. These were set alongside suite of 'handsome' Grecian couch, chairs and card tables and the 'handsome chimney glass'.[73] The relative modesty of pieces described as neat is still more apparent when we step outside at Braybrooke. In the coach-house, there was a 'handsome close carriage, in complete repair, with imperial and front & back seats' and also a 'neat single horse chaise (nearly new) & neat set of harness'. The larger, more imposing carriage is handsome; the smaller, lighter chaise is neat.

Handsome, elegant and neat all linked into notions of refined and polite taste, thus tying these second-hand goods and their clergy owners into wider value systems. It is significant that they played on notions of gentility, and on correctness and restraint, rather than emphasising the opulence and intrinsic luxury of the pieces. Only on rare occasions did adjectives obviously link to either the sensuous nature of luxury or ideas of splendour: 'rich' and 'splendid' are very sparingly used, appearing in only three gentry and two clergy catalogues, and nowhere do we see luxury or luxurious. Even with highly ornate and richly decorated pieces, the language remains restrained. At Crick, for example, a gilt china and ormolu lamp with an engraved glass shade was described as 'very elegant'.[74] The clergy were thus closely aligned with their gentry neighbours through the descriptions chosen by auctioneers who clearly saw parsonages, manor houses and even country houses occupying the same material world: one described and defined by the language of gentility.

## Conclusion

In presenting this analysis of the household goods of the rural clergy I do not pretend that all clergymen were the same. Some livings were far more valuable than others; combining them, a far from uncommon practice, could provide an income of several hundred pounds per annum and elevate the social standing of the incumbent. At the opposite end of the scale – and outside the bounds of this paper – were the curates, often employed by wealthy rectors and vicars to carry out some or all of their duties. It is scarcely surprising, then, that some of the houses studied here were grander and more handsomely furnished than were others. The rectories at Broughton, Orlingbury, Ecton and especially Crick were particularly large and the length of the auctions indicates the richness of their material culture – easily on a par with the houses of neighbouring gentry. That said, all of the rectors and vicars included in this study shared the same social world: one marked by gentility rather than mere respectability. Of itself, this is perhaps unsurprising, but the extent to which these men and their families enjoyed the material trimmings of gentility is remarkable: from the neat chaise in the coach house, to the elegant ormolu candlestick, to the handsome exoticism of a rosewood loo table. Significantly, this material world was more closely linked to notions of taste and inclusive sociability than to ostentatious displays of status through exclusive luxury objects. To be sure, these clergymen's drawing rooms and dining rooms were tastefully and richly furnished, but they were also comfortable and welcoming spaces where the furnishings allowed for informal sociability. In this, they were part of a more general shift in domestic culture and material culture, though whether we view it as new luxury, the rise of the informal house or the triumph of comfort is a matter of perspective. But gentility was not simply a product of the material objects themselves; it was also produced through the language deployed in the sale catalogues. Here we see the auctioneers who drew up these catalogues linking the clergymen's possessions to notions of refined taste and gentility through the ways in which they described the goods being sold. The chaise was neat, the ormolu candlestick was elegant and the loo table handsome.

Turning the argument around, what do these clergy houses tell us about gentility and about the ways in which material possessions were perceived and valued? Most obvious is the observation that gentility was, at least in part, materially defined. Possessing the domestic trappings of gentility did not necessary make these vicars and rectors gentlemen, but it did help to incorporate them into the same social, cultural and material world. It is important to note, however, that ownership was but the first step; gentility required assemblages of objects to create an active setting for refined social practices and their appropriate use in the changing rituals of polite sociability. In this, material possessions were not necessarily valued and valorised in terms of the novelty or fashionability, as much of the consumption literature would lead us to believe. Rather, it was the language of quality, workmanship and aesthetics that dominated. Whether we take auctioneers' descriptions at face value or as a sales pitch, they were clearly using language in a way that was attuned with their potential customers. Overall, then, gentility was defined and communicated through domestic goods, social practices and language – a web of interactions revealed vividly in the pages of auction catalogues.

## Notes

1 Northamptonshire Central Library (hereafter NCL), Sale Catalogue for Broughton rectory, 1790, M0005646NL/10.

2 B.A. Bax, *The English Parsonage* (London, 1964), pp. 102–4.

3 W. Bray, *Sketch of a Tour into Derbyshire and Yorkshire* (London, second edition, 1783),

4 J. Woodforde, *The Diary of a Country Parson, 1758–1802* (Norwich, 1999), p. 107.

5 See, for example, W. Sheils and D. Wood (eds), *The Church and Wealth* (Cambridge, 1987); W. Gibson, *The Achievement of the Anglican Church, 1689–1800* (Lewiston, 1995); Goldie, M., 'Voluntary Anglicans', *The Historical Journal*, vol 46 (2003).

6 Bax, *English Parsonage*; T. Brittain-Catlin, *The English Parsonage in the Early Nineteenth Century* (Reading, 2008); M. Ashby, 'Episcopal palaces in Georgian England: form, function and meaning' University of Cambridge PhD thesis, 2015.

7 L. Weatherill, *Consumer Behaviour and Material Culture in Britain, 1660–1760* (London, second edition, 1996), pp. 165–89.

8 W. Harrison, *The Description of England* (London, 1587), p. 197.

9 The classic studies include: N. McKendrick, J. Brewer and J. Plumb, *The Birth of a Consumer Society* (London, 1982); P. Earle, *The Making of the English Middle Class: Business, Society and Family Life in London 1660–1730* (Los Angeles, 1989); P. Langford, *A Polite and Commercial People: England 1727–1783* (Oxford, 1989); P.J. Corfield, *Power and the Professions in Britain, 1700–1850* (London: Routledge, 1995); M. Berg, *Luxury and Pleasure in Eighteenth-Century Britain* (Oxford, 2005);

10 See A. Hunt, *Governance of the Consuming Passions: History of Sumptuary Law* (Basingstoke, 1996); D. Roche, *The Culture of Clothing: Dress and Fashion in the Ancien Regime* (Cambridge, 1996); A. Pajur, 'The fabric of a corporate society: sumptuary laws, social order and propriety in early modern Tallin', in J. Ilmakunnas and J. Stobart (eds) *A Taste for Luxury in Early Modern Europe* (London, 2017), pp. 21–38.

11 Quoted in Earle, *Making of the English Middle Class*, p. 6. Many clergymen qualified on all of these fronts.

12 Examples of architectural treatises incorporating designs for parsonages include: W. Halfpenny, *Useful Architecture in Twenty-one new designs for Country Parsonages, Farm Houses and Inns* (London, 1752); J. Crunden, *Convenient and Ornamental Architecture . . .* (London: J. Taylor, 1788).

13 J. Stobart and M. Rothery, *Consumption and the Country House* (Oxford, 2016), 83–108; J. Whittle and E. Griffiths, *Consumption and Gender in the Early Seventeenth-Century Household* (Oxford, 2013), pp. 86–116.

14 T. Veblen, *The Theory of the Leisure Class: an Economic Study of Institutions* (1899; London: Penguin Classics Edition, 1994), p. 74. We need to be careful about taking Veblen's writing entirely at face value, but he rightly points to the importance of goods as social markers.

15 For discussion of the concept of luxury, see: Berg, *Luxury and Pleasure*, pp. 21–45; C. Berry, *The Idea of Luxury. A Conceptual and Historical Investigation* (Cambridge, 1994), pp. 138–9; L. Peck, *Consuming Splendor: Society and Culture in Seventeenth-Century England* (Cambridge, 2005), pp. 1–24.

16 Veblen, *Theory of the Leisure Classes*, p. 74.

17 W. Sombart, *Luxury and Capitalism* (Munich, 1913; English edition, Chicago, 1967), p. 105.

18 A. Vickery, *Behind Closed Doors. At Home in Georgian England* (New Haven, 2009), pp. 124–5. See also H. Grieg, 'Leading the fashion: the material culture of London's *beau monde*', in J. Styles and A. Vickery (eds), *Gender, Taste and Material Culture in Britain and North America 1700–1830* (New Haven, 2006), pp. 293–313

19 J. Stobart, 'Luxury and country house sales in England, *c*.1760–1830', in A. Fennetaux, A. Junqua and S. Vasset (eds), *The Afterlife of Used Things. Recycling in the Long Eighteenth Century* (London, 2015), pp. 25–36.

20 J. Stobart, 'Domestic textiles and country house sales in Georgian England', *Business History*, vol 61:1 (2019), pp. 17–37; W. Smith, *Consumption and the Making of Respectability, 1600–1800* (London: Routledge, 2002).

21 P. Edwards, *Horse and Man in Early Modern England* (London: Bloomsbury, 2007)

22 On the libraries of gentlemen and aristocrats, see M. Purcell, *The Country House Library* (London: Yale University Press, 2017).

23 NCL, Sale Catalogue for Rushton rectory, 1798, M0005646NL/17; Sale Catalogue for Crick rectory, 1836, M0005644NL/19.

24 NCL, Sale Catalogue for Crick rectory, 1836, M0005644NL/19; Sale Catalogue for East Farndon rectory, 1838, M0005644NL/22

25 Purcell, *Country House Library*, pp. 112–31.

26 NCL, Sale Catalogue for Crick rectory, 1836, M0005644NL/19, 39. On the bibliomania that encouraged such collecting, see Purcell, *Country House Library*, 160–79; one its spread beyond the elite, see I. Mitchell, *Tradition and Innovation in English Retailing, 1700 to 1850* (Farnham: Ashgate, 2014), pp. 119–24

27 NCL, Sale Catalogue for Ecton rectory, 1838, M0005644NL/24.

28 J. de Vries, *The Industrious Revolution: Consumer Behavior and the Household Economy, 1650 to the Present* (Cambridge: Cambridge University Press, 2008), pp. 44–5.

29 NCL, Sale Catalogue for Rolleston Hall, 1801, M0005647NL/2, 10.

30 NCL, Sale Catalogue for Cottingham, 1772, M0005644NL/2, 11; Sale Catalogue for Welton Place, 1830, M0005644NL/13, 17–18.

31 NCL, Sale Catalogue for Crick rectory, 1836, M0005644NL/19, Crick, 1836, 11; Sale Catalogue for Weldon rectory, 1761, M0005646NL/1, Weldon, 1761, 7.

32 NCL, Sale Catalogue for Crick rectory, 1836, M0005644NL/19, Crick, 1836, cover; M0005646NL/10, Broughton, 1790, 11, 19; M0005645NL/6, Orlingbury, 1824, 12.

33 NCL, Sale Catalogue for Little Bowden rectory, 1830, M0005645NL/14, 12; Sale Catalogue for Burton Latimer rectory, 1833, M0005645NL/20, 8.

34 Stratford Central Library and Archives, Receipted bill dated 6 November 1765, DR18/5/4385. See Stobart and Rothery *Consumption and the Country House*, p. 122.

35 De Vries, *Industrious Revolution*, pp. 44–5.
36 NCL, Sale Catalogue for Titchmarsh rectory, 1788, M0005646NL/8, 11.
37 NCL, Sale Catalogue for Ecton rectory, 1838, M0005644NL/24, 20–1.
38 Jean DeJean, *The Age of Comfort* (New York, 2009), pp. 131–9
39 K. Smith, 'In Her Hands: Materializing Distinction in Georgian Britain', *Cultural and Social History*, vol 11:4 (2014), pp. 489–506.
40 See Vickery, *Behind Closed Doors*, pp. 129–65; M. Ponsonby, *Stories from Home: English Domestic Interiors, 1750–1850* (Aldershot, 2007), pp. 25–33.
41 Berg, *Luxury and Pleasure*, pp. 21–45. This links to Appadurai's register of luxury – see A. Appadurai, 'Commodities and the politics of value', in A. Appadurai (ed.) *The Social Life of Things: Commodities in Cultural perspective* (Cambridge, 1986).
42 Smith, *Consumption and the Making of Respectability*, pp. 5–24.
43 NCL, Sale Catalogue for Titchmarsh rectory, 1788, M0005646NL/8; Sale Catalogue for Cranford St Andrew rectory, 1822, M0005645NL/3.
44 NCL, Sale Catalogue for Titchmarsh rectory, 1788, M0005646NL/8, 4.
45 NCL, Sale Catalogue for Islip Mills, 1787, M0005645NL/5.
46 J. Stobart, 'The language of luxury goods: consumption and the English country house, *c*.1760–1830', *Virtus*, 18 (2011), pp. 95–6.
47 NCL, Sale Catalogue for Crick rectory, 1830, M0005644NL/19, 7 & 15.
48 NCL, Sale Catalogue for Knuston Hall, 1809, M0005647NL/9, 12.
49 NCL, Sale Catalogue for Geddington House, 1823, M0005644NL/8, 1, 15, 16.
50 NCL, Sale Catalogue for Broughton rectory, 1790, M0005646NL/10, 10.
51 NCL, Sale Catalogue for Crick rectory, 1830, M0005644NL/19, 16; Sale Catalogue for Corby rectory, 1842, M0005645NL/23, 8–9; Sale Catalogue for Cranford St Andrew rectory, 1822, M0005645NL/3, 12.
52 NCL, Sale Catalogue for Titchmarsh rectory, 1788, M0005646NL/8, 6.
53 NCL, Sale Catalogue for Broughton rectory, 1790, M0005646NL/10, Broughton, 1790, 9.
54 See, inter alia, Berg, *Luxury and Pleasure*, pp. 46–84; T. Nechtman, *Nabobs: Empire and Identity in Eighteenth-Century Britain* (Cambridge, 2010); J. Eacott, *Selling Empire: India in the Making of Britain and America, 1600–1830* (Chapel Hill, 2016); M. Finn and K. Smith (eds), *The East India Company at Home, 1757–1857* (London, 2018).
55 NCL, Sale Catalogue for Ecton rectory, 1840, M0005644NL/24, 20–1 & 25.
56 On the impact of empire on the aesthetic and meaning of country houses, see S. Barczewski, *Country Houses and the British Empire, 1700–1930* (Manchester, 2014); S. Sloboda, *Chinoiserie: Commerce and Critical Ornament in Eighteenth-Century Britain* (Manchester, 2014); Finn and Smith, *East India Company at Home*.
57 Stobart, 'Language of luxury'.
58 C. Wall, *The Prose of Things: Transformations of Descriptions in the Eighteenth Century* (Chicago, 2006); Stobart, 'Luxury and country house sales'.
59 M. Berg 'New commodities, luxuries and their consumers in eighteenth-century England' in M. Berg and H. Clifford (eds.) *Consumers and Luxury* (Manchester, 1999), pp. 63–85
60 A. Vickery, *The Gentleman's Daughter. Women's Lives in Georgian England* (New Haven, 1998), p. 161.
61 Stobart, 'Language of luxury', pp. 97–8. This draws on ideas of speech-act theory. See J. Searle, *Speech Acts. An Essay in the Philosophy of Language* (Cambridge, 1969); J. Searle, 'A taxonomy of illocutionary acts', in K. Günderson (ed.), *Language, Mind, and Knowledge* (Minneapolis, 1975).

62 NCL, Sale Catalogue for Rushton rectory, 1809, M0005647NL/9, 14; Sale Catalogue for Ecton rectory, 1842, M0005644NL/24, 25.

63 NCL, Sale Catalogue for Corby rectory, 1842, M0005645NL/23, Corby, 1842, 7.

64 See C. Richardson, *A New Dictionary of the English Language* (London, 1839).

65 NCL, Sale Catalogue for Braybrooke rectory, 1828, M0005645NL/11, 4; Sale Catalogue for Lowick rectory, 1816, M0005647NL/16, 5.

66 NCL, Sale Catalogue for Crick rectory, 1830, M0005644NL/19, 10.

67 NCL, Sale Catalogue for Graton Underwood rectory, 1794, M0005646NL/12, 5; Sale Catalogue for Rothwell rectory, 1816, M0005647NL/17, 4; Sale Catalogue for East Farndon rectory, 1838, M0005644NL/22, 17.

68 See J. Barclay, *A Complete and Universal English Dictionary* (London, 1799).

69 Richardson, *New Dictionary*.

70 Barclay, *Complete and Universal English Dictionary*; Richardson, *New Dictionary*.

71 NCL, Sale Catalogue for Crick rectory, 1830, M0005644NL/19, 16–17.

72 Barclay, *Complete and Universal English Dictionary*; Vickery, *Behind Closed Doors*, pp. 180–2.

73 NCL, Sale Catalogue for Braybrooke rectory, 1828, M0005645NL/11, 4–5.

74 NCL, Sale Catalogue for Crick rectory, 1830, M0005644NL/19, 16.

# INDEX

ISBN 978-1-78683-714-1
eISBN 978-1-78683-715-8
ISSN (Print) 2057-4517
ISSN (Online) 2057-4525
*The Journal of Religious History, Literature and Culture*


FSC www.fsc.org MIX Paper from responsible sources FSC® C013604

***Contributors to*** *The Journal of Religious History, Literature and Culture* should refer enquiries to the journal page at www.uwp.co.uk or e-mail press@press.wales.ac.uk requesting notes for contributors.

***Advertising enquiries*** should be sent to the Sales and Marketing Department at the University of Wales Press, at the address below.

***Subscriptions:*** *The Journal of Religious History, Literature and Culture* is published twice a year in June and November. The annual subscription for institutions is £95 (print only), £85 (online only) or £140 (combined); and for individuals is £25 (print or online only) or £40 (combined). Subscription orders should be sent to University of Wales Press, University Registry, King Edward VII Avenue, Cardiff CF10 3NS. E-mail: press@press.wales.ac.uk.

***Open Access:*** The University of Wales Press (UWP) is fully committed to the principle of Open Access for those authors requiring it, whether by funder mandate, REF or otherwise. It is incumbent on contributors to state clearly if they have an Open Access requirement when submitting an article.

UWP's policy is to require an embargo period of eighteen months for Green Open Access, to begin on the last day in the month of publication of the print version. We also welcome submissions for Gold Open Access: if required, please contact the Commissioning Department at UWP to discuss an Article Processing Charge (APC) for your article.

The version of record for deposit should be the author's accepted and final peer-reviewed text, for non-commercial purposes.

The inclusion of third-party material in the deposited article will be at the author/institution's own risk. Authors should continue to ensure clearance of rights for third-party material for print and e-publication in the usual way for the purposes of the version published by UWP and for Open Access, if your article is Open Access.

UWP will continue to accept and publish articles by authors without requirements for REF under pre-existing arrangements.

For more information on our current Open Access policy, please visit our website: *www.uwp.co.uk/open-access*.